ID672595

LEE HARVEY
OSWALD

48 HOURS TO LIVE

SEP   2014

KHCPL MAIN
220 North Union St.
Kokomo, Indiana 46901-461
765.457.3242
www.KHCPL.org

OTHER BOOKS BY STEVEN M. GILLON

Pearl Harbor: FDR Leads the Nation into War

The Kennedy Assassination—24 Hours After

*The Pact: Bill Clinton, Newt Gingrich, and the Rivalry
That Defined a Generation*

10 Days That Unexpectedly Changed America

*Boomer Nation: The Largest and Richest Generation and
How It Changed America*

The American Paradox: A History of the United States Since 1945

The American Experiment: A History of the United States (vol. II)

*That's Not What We Meant to Do: Reform and
Its Unintended Consequences in Twentieth-Century America*

The Democrats' Dilemma: Walter F. Mondale and the Liberal Legacy

Politics and Vision: The ADA and American Liberalism, 1947–1985

LEE HARVEY OSWALD

48 HOURS TO LIVE

OSWALD, KENNEDY, AND THE CONSPIRACY THAT WILL NOT DIE

STEVEN M. GILLON

Scholar-in-Residence, HISTORY®
Professor of History, University of Oklahoma

HISTORY.

STERLING
New York

KOKOMO-HOWARD COUNTY PUBLIC LIBRARY
KOKOMO, IN

STERLING
New York

An Imprint of Sterling Publishing
387 Park Avenue South
New York, NY 10016

STERLING and the distinctive Sterling logo are registered trademarks
of Sterling Publishing Co., Inc.

HISTORY and the "H" logo are trademarks of A&E Television Networks, LLC
All rights reserved.

© 2013 by FernStreet, Inc.

See page 195 for photo credits

All rights reserved. No part of this publication may be reproduced,
stored in a retrieval system, or transmitted in any form or by any means
(including electronic, mechanical, photocopying, recording, or otherwise)
without prior written permission from the publisher.

ISBN 978-1-4549-1251-4

Distributed in Canada by Sterling Publishing
c/o Canadian Manda Group, 165 Dufferin Street
Toronto, Ontario, Canada M6K 3H6

Book design by Barbara Aronica-Buck

For information about custom editions, special sales, and premium
and corporate purchases, please contact Sterling Special Sales at
800-805-5489 or specialsales@sterlingpublishing.com.

Manufactured in the United States

2 4 6 8 10 9 7 5 3 1

www.sterlingpublishing.com

The book is dedicated to the Briarcliffe Athletic Association,
and to all of the coaches, especially John Crossan,
who made my childhood summers so magical and so meaningful.

ACKNOWLEDGMENTS

I could not have written this book without the support of the University of Oklahoma, the insight of many scholars and investigative journalists, and the encouragement of friends.

Gary Ginsberg read an early version of the book and offered a mix of thoughtful commentary and friendly encouragement.

Two graduate students at the University of Oklahoma were especially helpful. Eric England combed through thousands of pages of Warren Commission testimony and exhibits, providing me with a constant stream of information. Doug Miller offered his incisive commentary on an early draft.

At HISTORY™, my thanks to Kate Winn for agreeing to publish the book and to David Wilk for pulling it all together, and for doing so in record time.

The talented filmmaker Anthony Giacchino has once again turned written words into powerful images for a HISTORY® documentary. My thanks to associate producer R. Scott Frawley for tracking down pictures and artifacts for the project.

As always, I'm grateful to Abbe Raven and to Nancy Dubuc for all the opportunities they have provided me at the network.

CONTENTS

PREFACE

In October 1997, John F. Kennedy Jr. traveled to Havana to interview Cuban leader Fidel Castro for a feature in his new magazine, *George.* John often interviewed important historical figures for the magazine, but this interview was unlike any other. Castro sat down at a table and, with only an interpreter in the room, launched into a four-hour monologue about everything from the U.S. embargo, to civil rights, to world revolution. John never had a chance to utter a word. He listened; Castro lectured. John tuned Castro out in the first few minutes.[1]

The most revealing part of the meeting took place after the formal session had ended. As the two men exchanged farewells, Castro finally dropped his guard and tried to engage John in an informal, albeit, awkward, conversation. "How tall was your father?" Castro asked. "Was he as tall as you?" John, who was just a few days short of his third birthday when his father was assassinated, often confused his own memories of his father with the thousands of photos he had seen growing up. "I don't know," he responded. Knowing that Castro was his father's contemporary, John retorted: "You tell me."

As John was speaking, Castro moved closer, placed his hand on John's shoulder and leaned in as if he were about to share a secret. "You know," he said without prompting, "I could not have allowed Oswald into my country." Almost begging for John to acknowledge what he had just heard, Castro said: "You know that, don't you?" John did not say how he responded, but he thanked Castro for his time, shook his hand, and quickly made his way back to the United States.

Afterward, John interpreted Castro's comment as an awkward way of reassuring him that the Cubans had not been involved in his father's assassination. Not only was Oswald not a Cuban agent, he was not even welcome to enter the country. John, who rarely spoke about his father's death, seemed, on the surface at least, willing to accept Castro at his word. (In the fifteen-plus years that I knew him, John made only one passing mention of the conspiracy theories surrounding his father's death. "Bobby knew everything," he cryptically stated, suggesting that his uncle knew things that no one else did.*)

But Castro's comments are revealing on another level. American intelligence knew that a few weeks before the assassination Oswald had traveled to Mexico City where he bounced back and forth between the Cuban and Soviet embassies begging for an entrance visa. Both governments gave him the runaround and refused his request. It had long been speculated that while at the Cuban embassy Oswald threatened to kill President Kennedy. What has never been clear was whether the Cubans took those threats seriously. Castro's confession to John seems to confirm that the threat made its way all the way up the chain of command to Castro himself, and that the Cuban leader personally made the decision to deny a visa to the future assassin. Recent revelations lend further support to those claims.

Why are these revelations important? The new information about a possible, though tenuous, connection between Cuban intelligence and Oswald may help us understand his motives. They do not, as many conspiracy theorists have tried to assert, prove that Castro and the Cuban intelligence community masterminded the Kennedy assassination. Quite the contrary — Castro was too shrewd, and too masterful at the art of self-preservation, to conspire to assassinate the President of the United States. The retribution for such actions would have been devastating to him and to the revolution he so cherished. As Castro told John, he considered Oswald

---

* Robert F. Kennedy Jr. seemed to confirm those suspicions in a 2013 interview when he claimed that his father believed the Warren report was a "shoddy piece of craftsmanship." Robert F. Kennedy's oldest son said that his father "publicly supported the Warren Commission report but privately he was dismissive of it." His father suspected that the mob was behind the assassination and that more than one shooter was involved.

too much of a risk, but in recent years credible evidence has emerged that freelancing Cuban intelligence officials may have fanned Oswald's assassination fantasies.

Five decades after the assassination many Americans are still skeptical of the Warren Commission conclusion. Polls show that a majority of Americans, swayed by a vast army of conspiracy books and propaganda, refuse to believe that Oswald acted alone.

The skepticism is understandable. Are we to believe that ideology played no role in the plans of a former Marxist marine, who had once lived in the Soviet Union, to kill the president of the United States? That a man who could not hold a job, or even drive a car, could mastermind a daring midday assassination? And to top it off, are we to accept that Oswald's murder two days later at the hands of a local nightclub owner was a spontaneous act of outrage?

While this scenario seems implausible, it is far more convincing than any of the alternative explanations of the events in Dallas. It is the only theory that makes sense of most of the "known" facts, although when it comes to the Kennedy assassination it is difficult to find many facts upon which everyone agrees. I believe that the physical evidence proves that Oswald fired all of the shots at the presidential limousine on that fateful Friday afternoon. The question that lingers, and perhaps will never be answered with any certainty, is: Why?

Oswald took most of his secrets with him to his grave, but his actions in the final 48 hours of his life leave room for reasonable speculation about his motives. The final 48 hours of Oswald's life — beginning with assassination of President Kennedy at 12:30 p.m. on Friday afternoon and ending with Oswald's death at Parkland Hospital on Sunday afternoon — reveal a complicated figure. The pages that follow will try to peel back some of the layers of Oswald's personality and speculate about his motives and strategy. Was he a deranged loner searching for attention, or a misguided ideologue trying to make a statement? Or, as many have suggested, was he simply a pawn in a much larger plot to kill the president?

LEE HARVEY

OSWALD

48 HOURS TO LIVE

CHAPTER 1:

"Want to See a Secret Service Agent?"

On a typical morning, twenty-four-year-old Lee Harvey Oswald was up before the 6:30 a.m. alarm. He would reach over and hit the "off" switch so that the sound would not wake his two children, June and one-month-old Rachel, or disturb his Russian-born wife, Marina.

Friday morning, November 22, 1963, however, was different. Marina noticed that her husband had not slept well, and even after the alarm went off, he laid in bed for another ten minutes. Marina eventually turned to him and said, "Time to get up, Alka," using her Russian nickname for him. "Okay," he responded.[1]

Lee climbed out of bed, stretched his wiry 5'9" frame, washed, got dressed, and then returned to the bedroom. "Have you bought those shoes you are going to get?"

"No. I haven't had time."

"You must get those shoes, Mama. And, Mama, don't get up. I'll get breakfast myself."

Lee kissed the children, who were sleeping, but he did not kiss his wife goodbye. He turned and walked toward the bedroom door and then came back. "I've left some money on the bureau," he said in fluent Russian. "Take it and buy everything you and Junie and Rachel need."

Marina found his behavior unusual. Why would he tell her not to get up to make breakfast? She never made him breakfast. And why would he leave money for her and the children? He had never been so generous

before. When she got up later that morning she found $170, likely all the money that he had saved, on top of the bureau.[2]

Lee went to the kitchen and drank a cup of instant coffee. Before leaving he went into the garage and retrieved a package wrapped in brown paper and then walked the few blocks to where his coworker Buell Wesley Frazier lived with his sister. Since October, Lee had been living in a boarding house in Dallas while Marina and the children stayed with a friend in Irving. Lee usually hitched a ride from Frazier on weekends, but he surprised Marina by showing up on a weekday.

At 7:15 a.m. Frazier's sister, Linnie Mae Randle, peeked out her kitchen window and saw Lee approaching her house carrying a long brown package. She watched as he walked up to her brother's car, opened the right rear door, and carefully placed the package on the backseat. A few second later, Buell came out of the house and walked toward his 1959 Chevy four-door. He noticed that Lee was not carrying his lunch, which was usually contained in a brown paper bag. Spying the package on the back seat, he asked: "What's the package, Lee?"

"Curtainrods," Oswald responded.[3]

The two men rode in silence for the twenty-minute drive into downtown Dallas. A few minutes before 8:00 a.m., Frazier pulled up to the parking lot two blocks from the depository building where they worked. Oswald took the package from the backseat and walked toward the building.[4]

Oswald's job was to pick up orders for schoolbooks on the first floor, take the elevator to the fifth floor, locate the books, and bring them back down for packing and delivery. He tended to be a loner, rarely socializing with the other workers. On this morning he began his day by picking up the order form for three books: *Parliamentary Procedures*, ten copies of *Basic Reading Skills for High Schools, Revised*, and *Basic Reading Skills for Junior High Schools*. He placed the orders on his clipboard, climbed onto the elevator, and started up to the fifth floor.

There was an air of excitement in the building that day as most of the workers anticipated seeing President John F. Kennedy.

• • •

The president was on the second day of a two-day swing through a state that promised to be a major battleground in the 1964 presidential election. In 1960 Kennedy had carried the state by only 46,233 votes, even with native-son Lyndon Johnson on the ticket. Jackie Kennedy, the glamorous first lady, accompanied her husband on the trip — her first campaign appearance since the 1960 election.

Kennedy started his day at 8:45 a.m. standing in a misty rain in a Fort Worth parking lot. From there he moved inside for the main event — a breakfast meeting at the Hotel Texas for twenty-five hundred guests sponsored by the Chamber of Commerce. "Two years ago, I introduced myself in Paris by saying that I was the man who had accompanied Mrs. Kennedy to Paris. I am getting somewhat that same sensation as I travel around Texas," he said. "Nobody wonders what Lyndon and I wear."

At 10:35 a.m., the presidential party left their hotel for the short trip to Carswell Air Force base and the eight-minute flight to Dallas's Love Field airport. The president's political advisors decided to fly the thirty miles to Dallas so they could arrive in time for a midday motorcade through downtown to attract the largest possible crowds.

When the president and first lady stepped off the plane in Dallas "a great roar went up from thousands of throats." Presidential aide Dave Powers said they "looked like Mr. And Mrs. America." Jackie was wearing a pink wool suit with a matching pillbox hat. "Someone in the reception line added the final touch by presenting her with a bouquet of dark red roses," LBJ noted. "It all began so beautifully," recalled Lady Bird Johnson.[5]

At 11:55 a.m., President John F. Kennedy climbed into his car for the nine-and-a-half mile motorcade through Dallas en route to the Trade Mart, where he was scheduled to speak at a luncheon for local businessmen. To guarantee maximum exposure, Kennedy aides chose a circuitous route through the most populated parts of the city.

The motorcade, consisting of twenty-two cars, three buses, and over a dozen Dallas police motorcycles, extended more than a half mile. Dallas police chief Jesse Curry and two Secret Service agents were in the lead car. Five car lengths back was the presidential limousine, a specially designed twenty-one-foot long, midnight blue, seven-passenger Lincoln convertible, which carried the secret service designation SS 100X. Agent Bill Greer was

behind the wheel and Roy Kellerman sat to his right. Texas governor John Connally and his wife, Nellie, occupied the jump seats. President Kennedy sat directly behind the governor with Jackie to his left.

The president's advisors were feeling good about the motorcade. As they reached the downtown area, Kenneth O'Donnell marveled at the roaring crowds standing eight and ten deep, and hanging out the windows above. "There's certainly nothing wrong with this crowd," he said to Powers. Riding in the sixth car in the motorcade, Liz Carpenter, a Johnson press aide, turned to Jack Valenti, a local advertising executive who had helped organize the trip. "They do love this president, don't they?"[6]

• • •

Around noon, most of the employees at the book depository took their lunch break and went outside to get a glimpse of the president as the motorcade was to pass directly in front of their building. Oswald, however, remained inside, on the sixth floor. He started rearranging beige book cartons along the wall, using some of the larger book boxes to construct a four-and-a-half-foot wall. If anyone decided to enter the sixth floor, the wall would block their view of where Oswald was sitting. Inside the wall he placed smaller cartons that could be used to sit on. From the vantage point of the corner window, Oswald could see out across Dealey Plaza. He would be able to see the motorcade approaching along Houston Street, observe as it made a sharp left turn beneath him, and then continue to view it as it moved down the slope to the triple underpass.

After methodically moving boxes to prevent any other employees from seeing him, Oswald assembled a Mannlicher-Carcano Italian military rifle with a four-power scope that fired a 6.5 millimeter jacketed shell. Oswald had purchased the twenty-three-year-old rifle the previous March

by mail order from Chicago. He then sat on a small book box in his sniper's perch waiting for his prey. Occasionally he would stand with his rifle slung under his right arm, trying to get a look at the approaching motorcade. At 12:28 p.m. he would have seen the blinking red lights of the advancing motorcade and heard the sounds of police sirens.

At the top of Dealey Plaza, Howard L. Brennan, a forty-five-year-old steam fitter, stood facing the school book depository. Glancing up, he saw the beaming faces of men on the fifth floor. Above them he saw a young man holding a rifle. From what he could see he was in his early thirties, slender, probably 165 or 170 pounds, wearing light-colored clothes. It seemed odd to him, but he decided to mind his own business and keep his eyes trained on the presidential motorcade.

Standing a few feet away, another man looked up, saw the same sight, and then turned to his wife. "Want to see a Secret Service agent?" he asked, as he pointed to the young man holding a rife in the sixth-floor window. Ruby Henderson and Carolyn Walther looked at the same window and saw two men — one standing in the shadows, the other holding a rifle. Another bystander looked up and saw the man crouching in the window with his rifle pointed to the street below, but before having a chance to react he was distracted by the sound of the motorcade approaching the Plaza.[7]

At 12:30 p.m., as the presidential motorcade finished its turn onto Elm Street, Mrs. Connally flashed a smile and said: "Mr. Kennedy, you can't say the Dallas doesn't love you." The Secret Service called ahead to the Trade Mart telling them they would be there in five minutes.

Oswald peered through the scope and zoomed in on the back of President Kennedy's head.

•••

What brought Oswald to that sixth-floor window? The Warren Commission, while convinced Oswald was the lone shooter, remained agnostic about his motivation. "Many factors were undoubtedly involved in Oswald's motivation for the assassination, and the commission does not believe that it can ascribe to him any one motive or group of motives," it concluded.

Although it failed to ascribe a motive for the shooting, the Commission described a lonely, disaffected, sociopath who was in desperate need of attention. It spent a great deal of effort showing how the events in his childhood — growing up without a father, making few friends, and dealing with an overbearing mother — molded him into an angry, embittered misfit. A few of the people who met Oswald in the last two days of his life subscribed to this psychological interpretation of his actions. Detective James Leavelle, who observed Oswald's interrogations in the hours and days after the shooting, told the Sixth Floor Museum in 2002 that Oswald "was the type of individual that wanted to be somebody. He didn't shoot John F. Kennedy. He shot the president of the United States because that would get him notoriety and recognition."[8]

There is certainly a great deal of evidence to support Oswald's profile as a deranged sociopath. Born in New Orleans on October 18, 1939, he led a nomadic life as his self-absorbed mother, Marguerite, shuffled him between temporary homes and schools. Lee's biological father, Robert E. Lee Oswald, named after the famous Confederate general, died of a sudden heart attack two months before Lee was born. By that time, Marguerite was already thirty-two years old with two sons — John Pic, eight, from an earlier marriage, and Robert, who was five.

Moving often, unable to make friends, Lee became a loner, though one known for bouts of rage and violence. At thirteen, he underwent a psychological evaluation. Asked whether he preferred the company of boys or girls, Oswald told the psychiatrist, "I dislike everybody." Three years later, he dropped out of high school and joined the Marine Corps. Instead of providing him with discipline and direction, the Corps only exacerbated his psychological problems. During basic training in San Diego, he qualified as a sharpshooter. In October 1957, while assigned to an air base in Japan, he was court-marshaled for accidently shooting himself in the arm. A few months later, he was court-marshaled again for challenging a sergeant to fight. He served eighteen days in military prison.

The experience with military discipline left him even more bitter and withdrawn. Ironically, he found solace in communism. Although Oswald's fascination with Marxism dated back to high school, it intensified while in the Marine Corps. He started studying the Russian language, played

Russian music, and addressed his fellow Marines as "comrades." His behavior earned him the nickname: "Oswaldskovich."

In mid-August 1959, Oswald requested a discharge, claiming he needed to take care of his ailing mother. In reality he planned to defect to the Soviet Union. On his twentieth birthday he traveled to Moscow and announced his desire to become a Soviet citizen. When the Soviets rejected his request, Oswald slashed his wrists in a suicide attempt. The Soviets had little use for Oswald, but fearful that he might kill himself and create an international incident, they gave him permission to remain temporarily until a final decision could be made.

The Soviets sent him to work at a radio and television factory in Minsk, where he met Marina Prusakova, an attractive nineteen-year-old pharmacology student. They married in April 1961 and had their first child, June, the following February. Oswald assumed that as a former marine he would have been given special treatment. Rebuffed, he became disillusioned with the drudgery of Soviet life. In May 1962 he informed the U.S. Embassy that he was ready to come back home.

In June 1962, using a loan from the State Department, Oswald moved his family back to the United States. After arriving in Fort Worth, however, he became more withdrawn, irritable, and abusive. Marina complained to a neighbor that her husband was unable to support her and their child, and that he was sexually inadequate. At home Oswald acted like a tyrant, forbidding his wife from smoking, drinking, or wearing cosmetics. He refused to allow her to learn English, making her even more dependent on him.

Not only was Oswald becoming less emotionally stable and more ideologically rigid, he also revealed an extreme capacity for violence. Oswald had always been quick to anger. As a teenager, he had pulled a knife on his half brother's wife and even punched his mother in the face. His penchant for violence and his stridently ideological views seem to have come together in April 1963, when he attempted to assassinate right-wing retired general Edwin Walker. Using the same mail-order rifle that he carried into the book depository on November 22, Oswald fired at Walker from a distance of about one hundred feet as the general sat in his study. The bullet deflected off the window-frame, leaving Walker with a few bullet fragments in his forearm. Oswald fled the scene without being caught.

When he returned home late that evening he confessed to his wife that he had tried to kill the general, but cut her off before she could elicit an explanation. "Don't ask any questions," he instructed her. Marina, fearful that her husband would make another attempt, persuaded him to move to New Orleans.

In the final weeks of his life Oswald was preoccupied by Fidel Castro and by his desire to find a way to Cuba. "I only know that his basic desire was to get to Cuba by any means and all the rest of it was window dressing for that purpose," Marina said. He considered Castro a hero, and even considered naming his second child "Fidel." While in New Orleans, he opened a chapter of the Fair Play for Cuba Committee, which contained only one member: Oswald. He did manage to gain some local press attention when he got into a fight with anti-Castro Cubans. He also apparently made an effort to infiltrate anti-Castro groups, most likely in an effort to collect intelligence on their activities.[9]

On September 27, Oswald traveled to Mexico City where he shuttled back and forth between the Cuban Consulate and the Soviet embassy.

Oswald had once again grown disillusioned with life in America and planned to return to the Soviet Union (or perhaps stay in Cuba). While there are many conflicting reports about what took place — as there are with every aspect of Oswald's life — there seems to be some agreement on the basic narrative.[10]

Oswald's first stop was the Soviet Embassy, where CIA bugs captured him asking for entrance visas for him and his family. While at the embassy, Oswald claimed to have valuable information, and requested being placed somewhere on the Black Sea where the climate was warm. It is unclear what "hot" information Oswald had to trade, if any at all.[11]

The Soviets took some information from Oswald and then sent him to the Cuban Consulate, claiming he needed a transit visa that would allow him to fly from Mexico City to Cuba before going to the Soviet Union. But when he went to the Cuban embassy he was told the Soviets had to give him an entrance visa before they could give him a transit visa. He was getting the bureaucratic runaround. Oswald went back to the Soviet embassy and also made one final appeal to the Cubans. He carried a packet of materials to prove his loyalty to Fidel Castro and the Cuban revolution, including a card showing that he was a member of the Fair Play for Cuba Committee. Nothing worked.

Angry and frustrated that the Soviets had rejected his request, Lee returned to Dallas on October 4 and eventually took a room at a boarding house in Oak Cliff, a residential part of Dallas. By now, Marina was staying with a friend, Ruth Paine, and she had come to appreciate some of the comforts of living in her modest home in Irving, Texas. In early 1963 Oswald and Marina had met Ruth at a small party for a group of Russian émigrés. A young Quaker woman, Ruth was eager to learn the Russian language. She presented Marina with an attractive offer: Marina could live with her for free in return for providing Russian language sessions. Since Marina was pregnant with her second child, she welcomed the offer.

Ruth not only provided a room for Marina, she helped Lee find a job. She learned from her neighbor, Buell Wesley Frazier, about an opening at the book depository building. Lee applied and got the job. Beginning work on October 15, Lee filled book orders for $1.25 per hour. Four days later, Marina gave birth to their second daughter, Rachel. For the next few weeks, Oswald lived in his small boarding room from Monday through Friday, and then would hitch a ride to Irving with Frazier so he could spend the weekends with his family.

On November 19 the *Times Herald* published a detailed plan of the president's motorcade route, indicating that it would pass directly beneath the school book depository. Assuming that Oswald saw the paper that day, the earliest he could have started thinking about shooting the president was Tuesday.

On Thursday night, November 21, the evening before the assassination, Oswald made an unexpected trip to see Marina. That evening he begged her to return to him. He offered to rent a big new apartment and to fill it with some of the amenities she had become so accustomed to at the Paine house, namely a washer and dryer. Three times he asked; three times she refused. She was upset because she had learned that week that he was living under the false name of O.H. Lee. The lying and deception had to stop. "No," she said to herself, "if I don't teach him this lesson right now, this lying will continue. O.H. Lee will continue."[12]

By November 1963, Oswald found himself alone, living in a tiny room in an Oak Cliff boarding house, working a menial job as a stock boy. His world was collapsing around him. He had been disillusioned by the marines, by life in the Soviet Union, and now by his new life back in the United States. Cuban officials had denied his request to enter their country. His marriage was in trouble. Oswald was a trapped man. He needed to make some dramatic statement to shake things up.

Marina always wondered: If she had said yes, and accepted her husband's offer, would President Kennedy have left Dallas alive?

CHAPTER 2:

"Attention All Squads…Attention All Squads"

At 12:30 p.m., Oswald pulled the trigger. According to the Warren Commission, the first shot missed its mark. The second tore through President Kennedy's throat and struck Governor Connally in the back. "My God," Connally cried, "They're going to kill us all!" Nellie Connally pulled her husband into her lap and covered his body when a third shot struck, exploding Kennedy's head and showering her with blood, bone, and brains.[1]

There was never any doubt among those who witnessed the fatal third shot that Kennedy was dead. Secret Service agent Paul Landis, riding in the backup car, described the sound of the bullet hitting Kennedy's head as "the sound you would get by shooting a high-powered bullet into a five-gallon can of water or shooting into a melon." The result was devastating. "I saw pieces of flesh and blood flying through the air and the President slumped out of sight toward Mrs. Kennedy." "My immediate thought was that the President could not possibly be alive after being hit like he was," Landis testified. Another agent, Clint Hill, ran toward the car and leaped onto the back of the limousine. He looked at the president's wound and gave a thumbs-down signal with his hand. After watching the third bullet explode Kennedy's head, Kenneth O'Donnell blessed himself. He knew that his friend was dead.[2]

Within seconds, the presidential limousine was racing to the hospital. "We were floating in yellow and red roses and blood," recalled Nellie Connally. "It was a sea of horror." In the back seat, Jackie cradled her husband's body. "All the ride to the hospital I kept bending over him saying 'Jack, Jack, can you hear me. I love you Jack. I kept holding the top of his head down trying to keep the brains in." [3]

• • •

As soon as word reached Washington that the president had been shot, the CIA set up a "Watch Committee" that monitored foreign intelligence and assembled information from every possible source. "We all went to battle stations," recalled Richard Helms, chief of the Agency's covert operations. "It worried the hell out of everybody. Was this a plot? Who was pulling the strings? And what was to come next?" At the Pentagon, Secretary of Defense Robert McNamara called the chairman of the Joint Chiefs of Staff, General Maxwell Taylor, and suggested that they place all troops on alert because they did not know whether a foreign power had been involved in the shooting. [4]

• • •

After firing the third shot, Oswald slipped between the cartons of books and hurried toward the rear staircase. Oswald clearly had no intent of being a martyr. He wanted to get away from the crime scene before police swarmed the building. He likely had not anticipated just how much confusion the shots would have created as they echoed around the plaza and led some people to believe they came from the grassy knoll that was to the front, right of JFK's automobile. He dropped the rifle into an opening between several large boxes near the stairs, and then ran down the stairs until he heard the sound of footsteps coming in his direction. He exited onto the second floor and went into a lunchroom. There he was confronted by Dallas policeman Marrion Baker.

A motorcycle policeman riding in the motorcade behind the president's car, Baker heard the shots coming from the book depository. When he looked up he saw a flock of pigeons fly off the roof. With his pistol drawn, he raced to the front of the building. "Who's in charge here?" he called out. Building manager Roy Truly, who was standing in front of the depository at the time of the shooting, saw Baker run inside the building. Realizing that Baker did not know the floor plan, Truly offered to guide him to the higher floors.[5]

The two men dashed up the narrow wooden stairs. On the second floor they encountered a calm Lee Harvey Oswald in the lunchroom. "Come here," he said, pointing his gun at Oswald. As Oswald made his way closer, the officer asked Truly, "This man work here?" "Yes," he responded, "he works for me." The officer quickly turned and continued up the stairs. Had Truly not intervened, or if the officer had asked a few more questions (why did he assume that the shooter would not be someone who worked in the building?) Oswald would have been caught then.[6]

After his confrontation with Baker, Oswald purchased a Coke from a vending machine. A colleague encountered Oswald near the second floor stairwell still holding the bottle of soda in his hands. "Isn't it terrible?" she said. Oswald mumbled a response but seemed strangely disengaged from what had just taken place.[7]

After the encounter, Oswald continued down the last flight of steps and walked out the front door of the depository. He was outside in less than three minutes.

As Oswald left the building a well-dressed man with a crew cut, displaying some kind of credentials, approached Oswald and asked, "Where is the telephone?" (It was NBC's Robert MacNeil, who was desperately searching for a phone to call in his report.) Oswald, who believed the man was a Secret Service agent, responded, "Right there," pointing to a phone inside the building. As MacNeil rushed past him, Oswald began walking away from the scene of the crime.[8]

As he fled, police converged on the building. At 12:34 p.m. the police dispatcher mentioned the book depository as a possible source of the shots. One minute later, a motorcycle policeman radioed that he had "talked to a guy who says the shots were fired from the Texas School Book Depository."[9]

• • •

At 12:36 p.m., the presidential motorcade reached Parkland Hospital. As soon as they arrived, Secret Service agents removed JFK's lifeless body from the bloodstained limousine, placed him on a stretcher, and rushed him into the hospital where a team of doctors was waiting for him in emergency room 1.

Had he been just another patient, doctors would have declared Kennedy "dead on arrival." "We never had any hope of saving his life," said Dr. Malcolm Perry. The president had no pulse. His skin was cool to the touch. His color was "blue white, ashen." Brain matter and tissue were oozing from the massive open wound in the back of his head. He was, however, the president of the United States, so the team of doctors engaged in a herculean, but futile, effort to save his life. "He had a death look," recalled Dr. Pepper Jenkins, one of the doctors who first viewed the president's body. "He was on the way out."[10]

The prognosis for Governor Connally was more optimistic. Approximately ten minutes after he had been brought into the hospital, doctors transferred the governor to an operating room on the second floor. He had suffered serious wounds that required extensive surgery, but doctors expected him to survive.

• • •

While the police converged on the book depository building and doctors began working on JFK, Oswald was briskly walking the seven blocks from the depository building to the bus stop at Elm and Murphy. At 12:40 p.m., he boarded a bus driven by Cecil McWatters. Oswald did not realize it, but a former landlady, Mary Bledsoe, was also on the bus and recognized him immediately. "He looks like a maniac," she observed. [11]

At just the time that Oswald stepped on the bus, the Secret Service placed a frantic call for a priest to administer the last rites of the Roman Catholic Church to the mortally wounded president.

With all of the police activity in the area around Dealey Plaza, traffic had come to a standstill. At 12:44 p.m., Oswald asked for a transfer, got off the bus, crossed in front of it, and started walking to the Greyhound bus station, which was three and a half blocks away.

As he proceeded, police began broadcasting a description of the shooter based on Howard Brennan's eyewitness account. The description matched Oswald (and hundreds of other young men in Dallas). "Attention all squads. Attention all squads. At Elm and Houston, reported to be an unknown white male, approximately 30, slender build, height 5'10", 165 pounds. Reported to be armed with what is believed to be a .30-caliber rifle."[12]

A dispatcher ordered police car #10 to patrol the Oak Cliff area. The driver was J.D. Tippit, an eleven-year veteran of the force. The Dallas police had recently begun experimenting with the new policy of allowing officers to ride alone in cars patrolling low-crime areas. Tippit had voted for Kennedy and he would have liked to have seen him, but he was also relieved to be far removed from the dangerous and high-stakes job of guarding his safety. "10-4," Tippit radioed back. [13]

At 12:47 p.m., Oswald entered a taxi driven by William Whaley at the Greyhound Bus Terminal. Whaley opened the back door for his passenger, but Oswald said he wanted to sit in the front seat — a common practice in the Soviet Union. Oswald told him to take him to the 500 block of North Beckley. While he was riding in the cab, police once again broadcast a description of the shooter to all cruisers. Whaley, who had not yet heard the news, asked his passenger about all the police sirens. Oswald did not respond. He rode the entire way in silence. The driver thought Oswald was "a wino two days off the bottle."[14]

After the two-and-a-half mile ride Oswald asked the driver to drop him off at Beckley and Neely, about a ten-minute walk from his boarding house. Why not have the driver take him right to his house? Oswald likely feared that police would have already identified him as the killer and were speeding to his room. He wanted to spy on the area and make sure it was safe. "This will do," he said. The driver pulled over to the curb. The fare was ninety-five cents. Oswald handed the driver $1. "Keep the change," he said.[15]

• • •

At 12:50 p.m., while Oswald was walking to his room, doctors stopped working on JFK. They stepped aside to allow the Reverend Oscar Huber to perform the last rites. He held up his right hand and began the prayer in Latin, which translated. "If you are living, I absolve you from your sins. In the name of the Father and of the Son and of the Holy Ghost. Amen." He then reached into his pocket and pulled out a vial of holy oil. He placed a small amount on his right thumb and the made the sign of the cross on President Kennedy's forehead. "Through this holy anointing may God forgive you whatever sins you may have committed. Amen."[16]

It took Oswald nine minutes to make it to the rooming house. The housekeeper, Earlene Roberts, had just learned that the president had been shot when she saw the front door swing open and Oswald come in. "Oh, you are in a hurry," she said. He ignored her comment, moved quickly past her and into his small room to the left of the living room. There were double doors leading into what had once been a small alcove. The room was about five by twelve feet with the bed taking up most of the space. An air conditioner occupied one of the four adjacent windows, which were screened by venetian blinds and lace curtains.

.38 Caliber Smith & Wesson Revolver
Commission Exhibit 143
FBI Exhibit C15

Although it was a warm day, Oswald pulled a white "Eisenhower" jacket from the rack, tucked a revolver into the waistband of his pants, and rushed out of the house. He spent a total of four minutes in the house.[17]

During those four minutes, doctors at Parkland Hospital doctors officially declared JFK dead. Shortly after 1:00 p.m., Attorney General Robert Kennedy received a phone call at his home in Virginia informing him that the wounds his brother suffered proved fatal.[18]

Back at the book depository the supervisor told police that one of his employees was missing. His name: Lee Harvey Oswald.

• • •

Oswald left the boarding house at 1:03 p.m., zipping up his jacket to hide his pistol as he walked out the door. Where was he headed? It is clear that his was not a suicide mission. Oswald set up the shooting to allow himself an easy escape (at least as easy an escape as possible from the sixth floor of a building in a crowded downtown area swarming with law enforcement officials). He had a direct frontal shot at the president as his motorcade moved toward the book depository building on Houston Street. Instead, Oswald allowed the car to make the sharp left turn so he could shoot the president from behind, confusing the secret service, and allowing an opportunity to escape.

But escape to where? It is impossible to know for sure, but there are a several possibilities. Some conspiracy theorists have speculated that Oswald planned to meet with his "handlers" at the Texas Theatre where he was to be eliminated as part of a larger plot. (When that failed, "they" sent Ruby to do the job two days later). Of course, those who maintain Oswald's innocence accept the version he later told police. He was not in a hurry to go anywhere: he left the building after the shooting because he assumed the building would be closed. He went home, grabbed his gun, and went to the theater.

There are a few other scenarios that fall into the same highly improbable category. Some have suggested that Oswald was on a mission that day and that JFK was only his first target. Congressman Harold Sawyer, a Michigan congressman and member of the House Select Committee on Assassinations, suggested that Oswald grabbed his handgun to kill a man who had been identified in the Dallas press as a communist informer. According to Sawyer the man lived only a few blocks from where Oswald shot Officer Tippit. There have also been suggestions that Oswald was headed to finish off General Walker.[19]

A second school of thought, closely associated with those who support the general conclusions of the Warren Commission, maintains that Oswald had no plan and was simply improvising. According to Jean Davidson, author of *Oswald's Game*, Oswald never expected to get out of the book depository alive. "He probably assumed that the building would have been surrounded much more quickly than it was and he never would have gotten out of the building alive," she reflected. He simply did not have time to plan an escape route. Oswald only learned two days earlier that the president would be going past the book depository building. If he had given some thought to the escape he would have anticipated that a city bus would have been trapped in the chaos that he had created. "A city bus is not the usual means of escape if someone had planned ahead of time," she pointed out.[20]

Other serious students of the assassination share this view. John McAdams, the creator of a conspiracy debunking website, the Kennedy Assassination Homepage, believes that Oswald had not given serious thought to getting away. "It looks to me like he has improvising," he told the author. "He never expected to get out of the book depository building without being captured or killed." According to this view, once Oswald left the crime scene and managed to get back to the boarding house to retrieve his pistol, he was lost. "He was just walking around Oak Cliff trying to decide what to do before the police caught him," recalled McAdams. [21]

A third school supports the Warren Commission's conclusions, but speculates that Oswald had an escape plan after the shooting. Gerald Posner, author of *Case Closed,* concluded that Oswald likely "had a plan for how to get out of Dallas." Posner believes that Oswald "was on his way back to Mexico City and the Cuban consulate." This is a view shared by journalist Max Holland, who also believes that Oswald was the lone assassin.[22]

Oswald "didn't want to go back to Russia any longer," Posner told the author in 2012. "He only wanted to get to Cuba where he thought the real revolution was happening. These were the same bureaucrats who refused him a visa to Havana only a month earlier. He intended to show up and say, 'This is what I've done,' and they would have no choice but to enthusiastically embrace him."[23]

Oswald, it turned out, had just enough money in his pocket to pay for a one-way bus trip to Mexico City. In an unpublished draft of the Warren Commission, counsel David Belin suggested that Oswald was only four blocks from catching a Route 55 bus that would have taken him to Lancaster Road, where he could have boarded a southbound Greyhound bus that would have, with connections, traveled to Monterrey, Mexico.[24]

Just as his motives were complicated, so were Oswald's movements after the shooting. It is impossible for any single theory to explain all the contradictions of his actions. If Oswald were planning to take a bus to Mexico why not take one from the main bus terminal downtown? He did not even enter the building, and instead grabbed a taxi outside. Also, he would have needed a visa to cross the border. How was he planning to get into Mexico? Finally, he had enough money to pay for the bus ticket, but how was he planning to survive once he reached Mexico?

There are plausible responses to these questions. He likely wanted to avoid the central bus terminal because he assumed the police would be looking for him there; better to get a bus a little further out of town. The lack of a visa is harder to explain. Maybe he thought he could talk his way over the border. Of course, it is just as likely that he believed that someone was going to help him get to Mexico City. Given that he had barely enough money to pay for the bus ticket, and that he had left his entire savings with Marina, it would appear that he expected to be taken care of once he crossed the border.

Former CIA analyst Brian Latell believes that the offers of assistance may have come from Cuban intelligence. If Cuban intelligence had been involved with Oswald, they would have either assigned a dedicated agent in Dallas or a "cut up" — someone personally loyal to Castro but with no official status. A dedicated agent would have been authorized to make promises and to provide Oswald with assistance getting out of Dallas and the United States. A "cut up" would have no such official authority, but could still have offered aid. In either case, Oswald would have had support and encouragement from an outside source, and assistance getting across the border.

This explanation still begs the question of why Castro would take the risk of being tied to someone trying to assassinate the president of the United States when he knew it would be suicide if Oswald were caught. Latell speculates that it is most likely that Cuban intelligence officers were freelancing; that Castro would not have been aware of their efforts to encourage Oswald to follow through on his threat against Kennedy's life.

It seems unlikely, however, that low-level Cuban operatives would have taken on such a risky operation without Castro's knowledge, and even less likely that the Cuban leader would have sanctioned such an operation. Despite the lack of physical evidence, and the heavy weight of logic against this theory, Latell is highly credible and not easily dismissed as a conspiracy crackpot. If he is right, the elusive final answers to the Kennedy assassination are probably locked away collecting dust in a secure Cuban intelligence archive.

Whether Oswald was improvising, or he was trying to get across the border with or without the help of Cuban intelligence, he certainly had not expected to run into Dallas police officer J. D. Tippit.

CHAPTER 3:

"Somebody Shot a Police Officer"

At approximately 1:15 p.m., as JFK's close aide Kenneth O'Donnell informed vice president Lyndon Johnson that the president was dead, Dallas patrolman J.D. Tippit pulled onto Tenth Street in central Oak Cliff. A few minutes earlier a radio dispatcher had told Tippit to be available "for any emergency that comes in." Given that he was three miles away from the assassination scene at Dealey Plaza, it probably seemed unlikely that any emergency would come his way. But he would likely have heard the description of the suspect in the shooting — and probably more than once.

Tippit's actions in the minutes before he encountered Oswald are something of a mystery. At 1:03 p.m. Tippit failed to respond to the police dispatcher, who had called to ask for his location. Witnesses, who saw Tippit sitting in his squad car at a gas station watching traffic coming out of downtown Dallas, claimed that he left in a hurry at 1:06 p.m. — just a few minutes after Oswald walked out of his boarding house. Five minutes later, two credible witnesses claim they saw Tippit enter the Top Ten Record Shop, where he used the local pay phone. He never said a word, and exited just as quickly. We will never know why Tippit entered the store, whom he was trying to call, or why he was in such a hurry. What we do know is that he had only a few minutes to live.[1]

Tippit spotted a man who fit the police description walking swiftly along the sidewalk on the south side of Tenth Street just past the Patton Street intersection. It's possible that Oswald turned and started walking in the opposite direction in an effort to avoid Tippit. The sudden move may have attracted the officer's attention. Taxi driver W. W. Scoggins was sitting in his parked car eating his lunch on the east side of Patton. Helen Markham, a waitress at the Eat-Well Cafe in downtown Dallas, was standing on the northwest corner of Tenth and Patton on her way to catch a bus.

Tippit pulled up behind Oswald and called him over. According to witnesses, Oswald leaned into the passenger window of Officer Tippit's car as the two men spoke. Whatever Oswald said apparently did not satisfy Tippit, who got out of the car and started walking around to continue his questioning. Just as Tippit reached the front driver's side tire, Oswald pulled out his revolver and fired. Tippit was hit four times: two bullets to the chest, one to the forehead, and one to the temple. Oswald then "just walked calmly, fooling with his gun." Waitress Markham rushed to the officer's side, screaming hysterically, "He shot him! He is dead! Call the police!"[2]

After shooting Tippit, Oswald walked toward Scoggins, who was sitting in his taxi. As Oswald approached, Scoggins climbed out of his car and crouched along the side to avoid being seen. Oswald walked quickly past him and fled the scene. "Poor dumb cop," he heard Oswald mutter.

Inside a small house in front of the police car, sisters-in-law Barbara and Virginia Davis witnessed Oswald darting across their lawn with a pistol in his hand. He cut through Patton Street to West Jefferson Boulevard, emerging by a Texaco Station across from a parking lot where he dropped his jacket. He then walked past a car dealer where two men, Ted Callaway and Sam Guinyard, saw him still holding his gun.[3]

At 1:16 p.m., Temple Ford "Thomas" Bowley, who had just picked up his daughter from school, drove up to the scene of the shooting. He rushed to Tippit's side, turned him over (he was laying on his side), and knew immediately that he was beyond help. He then used the police radio to say, "Hello, police operator — we've had a shooting out here . . ." Within a few minutes police cars were speeding toward the scene of the murder, and they now had detailed descriptions of the killer.[4]

At 1:19 p.m., four minutes after the shooting, the dispatcher announced that "the subject is running west on Jefferson from the location." The police broadcast a fresh and accurate description of Oswald based on two witnesses to Tippit's murder.[5]

The shooting of Officer Tippit changed the game for Oswald. If he had an escape plan it likely did not include a chance encounter with a Dallas police officer miles from the scene of the assassination. When he shot the president he had the advantage of cover. He killed Tippit on a street with numerous witnesses. There were no crowds of people to blend into; no mass confusion to provide cover. Within minutes police cars were searching the area. There were few places to hide. Before pulling the trigger on his pistol, Oswald could fancy himself a revolutionary. Murdering Kennedy may have had both ideological and practical implications — it would allow him to slay Castro's enemy and, perhaps, provide a ticket to Cuba. Now he was just a cop killer.

• • •

Police were now working two crime scenes. As they raced to the scene of the Tippit murder, detectives at the book depository building were busy uncovering evidence that would eventually connect Oswald to the assassination of President Kennedy. By 1:22 p.m. they had discovered the shooter's nest on the sixth floor, with three empty shells on the floor, and had began dusting for prints. They also found an old rifle tucked away behind boxes just a few feet from the rear stairway.

• • •

As Oswald fled the scene of the Tippit murder, LBJ was preparing to leave Parkland Hospital. At 1:26 p.m., the secret service formed a phalanx around President Johnson and rushed him out through the ambulance bays. The Secret Service had lined up two unmarked police cars for the trip. In order to help confuse a potential assassin they decided that the president and Mrs. Johnson ride in separate cars. Johnson slumped into the back seat of the lead car as police chief Jesse Curry manned the wheel.

A few minutes after Johnson left Parkland Hospital, White House assistant press secretary Malcolm Kilduff walked into the makeshift press room. At 1:33 p.m., holding a piece of paper in one hand and an unlit cigarette in the other, Kilduff stood in front of the classroom blackboard and read the statement: "President John F. Kennedy died at approximately one o'clock Central Standard Time today here in Dallas. He died of a gunshot wound in the brain. I have no other details regarding the assassination of the president. Mrs. Kennedy was not hit. Governor Connally was not hit. The vice president was not hit."* Two minutes later, United Press International teletype machines around the world reported: "FLASH President Kennedy Dead."

Walter Cronkite made the announcement on CBS. "From Dallas, Texas, the flash, apparently official. President Kennedy died at 1:00 p.m. Central Standard Time, two o'clock Eastern Standard Time." He paused for a moment and looked at the studio clock. "Some thirty-eight minutes ago." Fighting back tears, Cronkite removed his eyeglasses and cleared his throat.

• • •

Among those watching events unfold on television was Jack Ruby. Born Jacob Rubenstein on Chicago's tough West Side, Ruby dropped out of high school and picked up odd jobs before being drafted into the army in 1943. After the war he traveled to Dallas where he helped manage a nightclub owned by his sister, Eva. Shortly after he arrived in 1947 he changed his name to Ruby. His first few ventures failed, but eventually he achieved some success with the Carousel Club.

A stocky 5'8" and 175 pounds, Ruby had earned a reputation around town as a quick-tempered, sometimes violent bully. He was known for his explosions of violence, and lost the tip of his left index finger when someone bit it off in a fight. He served as the unofficial bouncer for his own clubs, and sent more than a few customers to the hospital. He was unpredictable: angry and violent one minute, jovial and friendly the next.

Ruby worked hard to ingratiate himself to members of the Dallas police and he had plenty of opportunities. He was arrested nine times for minor infractions. Many other officers knew him because his clubs were on their beat and they had been interacting with him for years.

He desperately wanted to be known as a "big man" in Dallas, but most people viewed him as little more than an annoying character. He always

---

* Reporters would soon discover that Kilduff had misspoken when he said that Connally was not hit.

had businesses on the side, selling everything from costume jewelry to sew-ing machine attachments, vitamins, twist boards, and razor blades. "Jack Ruby was the quintessential wanna-be but never-was," observed veteran Dallas newsman Hugh Aynesworth. "Full of big stories, bigger dreams and lusty braggadocio, the strip show operator was first and foremost a lowlife, a man who searched for class as though he understood what it was. . . . Hardly a week went by in Dallas when you wouldn't see Ruby promot-ing some inane product, chasing fire trucks, pushing himself into public displays or passing out his Carousel Club calling cards at the fights, in the bars, or on downtown streets."

On the morning of November 22, Ruby, dressed in a dark suit and wearing diamond pinkie rings, stood in the office of the *Dallas Morning News*, which was only five blocks from Dealey Plaza. He drove there to place an ad promoting his Carousel Club. While waiting he began browsing the morning paper and came across an entire page with large black letters, exclaiming "Welcome Mr. Kennedy to Dallas." It was anything but welcoming, however. It accused Kennedy of being a communist tool and was signed by "the American Fact-Finding Committee, Bernard Weissman, chairman."

Ruby thought the ad was offensive on a number of levels. He found it disrespectful of the president, especially on a day that he was visiting the city. Ruby had little interest in politics, and although he admired Kennedy, he had not planned to see him. He thought his visit was good for the city and believed that people should rally around him, if only for a day. It also upset him that the person running the ad had a Jewish name. Ruby was part of a small Jewish community in Dallas, and he was sensitive about being part of a minority group in an overwhelmingly Protestant state. He even suspected that the ad's author was not Jewish at all, but instead someone who was trying to give Jews a bad name. [6]

As he was reading the ad two employees ran into the office and announced that shots had been fired at the president's motorcade. According to one witness, Ruby exhibited a look of "stunned disbelief," and was "emotionally upset." He sat there "staring unbelieving at the television set," said one witness. "He was virtually speechless, quite unusual for Jack Ruby."

Jack Ruby turned pale and started crying when the announcement came that Kennedy was dead. He called his sister Eva from the newsroom. She said that he cried harder that day then he had at his parents' funeral.[7]

The Warren Commission concluded that Ruby left the *Dallas Morning News* a few minutes after the Cronkite announcement and returned to his club, but Gerald Posner has speculated that he may have gone to Parkland Hospital. Despite his grief, Ruby always had to be near the center of action. Seth Kantor, a reporter who had been traveling with the president, recalled running into Ruby in the stairwell. "Ruby called me by my first name and I grasped his extended hand. He looked miserable. Grim. Pale. There were tears brimming in his eyes."[8]

• • •

Fidel Castro was also carefully monitoring news reports from Dallas. Journalist Jean Daniel was having lunch at the Cuban leader's home on

Varadero Beach outside Havana when the telephone rang with an urgent message. Fidel picked up the phone and said, in Spanish, "What's that? An attempted assassination?" He was told that Kennedy had been seriously wounded. According to Daniel, Castro sat down next to him and kept muttering, "This is bad news." He speculated out loud about who could have been responsible for such an act: the Klu Klux Klan? The Vietnamese? A terrorist cell in the United States? A second call came in suggesting that doctors were working on Kennedy and might be able to save his life. Castro's reaction: "If they can, he is already re-elected."

The two men, along with an aide, tuned into radio broadcasts from an NBC station in Miami while the aide translated the broadcasts for Fidel. The story unfolded quickly: The president had been shot in the head; police were in pursuit of his assassin; a Dallas policeman had been murdered; Kennedy was dead. Upon hearing the news of Kennedy's death, Castro stood up: "Everything is changed. Everything is going to change," he said. "Now," Fidel said, "they will have to find the assassin quickly, but very quickly, otherwise, you watch and see, I know them, they will try to put the blame on us for this thing."[9]

* * *

Oswald was now desperate to avoid capture. When he saw police cars coming up Jefferson Street, he turned his back and ducked into the foyer of Hardy's Shoe Shop. Assistant manager Johnny Brewer, twenty-three, who had heard radio reports about JFK's death, thought Oswald looked suspicious. He appeared to be avoiding the police cars that were speeding past with their sirens blasting. Brewer decided to follow him.

About fifty yards from the shoe store, and eight blocks from the Tippit murder scene, stood the Texas Theatre, which was open for a matinee showing of two new films, *Cry of Battle* and *War Is Hell.* Oswald walked past the cashier, who had stepped out of the booth and was standing on the sidewalk. Brewer walked up to the clerk and pointed out that a man had ducked into the theater without paying the ninety-cent charge.

Some conspiracy theorists have speculated that the theater may have been a prearranged meeting place, but it is more likely that a desperate

Oswald was simply trying to avoid capture and a dark movie theater seemed like a good place to hide.

At 1:40 p.m., the clerk called the police about a suspicious-looking man who had just entered the theater and wondered whether he might be the person responsible for shooting the president. After she described him, the dispatcher responded, "Well he fits the description."

At 1:45 p.m., the dispatcher announced: "Have information a suspect just went in the Texas Theatre on West Jefferson." A few minutes later six squad cars, containing sixteen police officers, sealed the theater's front and rear exits.

CHAPTER 4:

"Well, It Is All Over Now"

At 1:50 p.m. Officer Jerry Hill came in through the front door of the Texas Theatre and ordered the manager to turn on the house lights. Hill was soon joined by Officer Paul Bentley. "Come on, Paul," Hill said. "Let's try the balcony." The two men rushed to the balcony where they found six youngsters playing hooky from school.[1]

Johnny Brewer entered the back of the theater escorted by four policemen. He scanned the theater and saw Oswald sitting in a back center row, a few seats from the aisle. Officers "Nick" McDonald and C. T. Walker left the stage walking up the left aisle; T. A. Hutson and Ray Hawkins took the right aisle. As McDonald made his way up the aisle a man near the front told him that the person he was looking for was seated in the third row from the rear. The officer continued up the aisle, crouching low with his gun drawn. When he reached Oswald's aisle McDonald shouted, "On your feet!"

Oswald slowly stood up, raised both hands, and then yelled, "Well, it is all over now." He punched the police officer in the face, and pulled his pistol from his pants. McDonald grabbed Oswald around the waist as the two men fell into the seats. The officer managed to get his hand on the gun handle. Oswald still had his finger on the trigger and tried shooting. McDonald heard the hammer click. The primer, which fires the bullet, was dented, but for some reason did not fire. "This might have saved me," McDonald wrote in an account of the capture published in the *Dallas Morning News* on Sunday, November 24.[2]

Other officers jumped into the scuffle and wrestled Oswald to the ground. There was confusion as Oswald and a handful of officers rolled on the ground in the narrow aisle. At one point they thought he was handcuffed, but the police had accidently linked Oswald's hand to that of another officer. Detective Bentley jumped on top of Oswald and hit him with his ring finger on the side of the head above his eye, giving him the distinctive black eye he would wear for the next two days.

Once the officers had disarmed and handcuffed Oswald, they lifted him to his feet. According to author Bishop, Oswald was calling the officers "Sons of bitches!" and "Bastards." An officer tried to silence him by punching him in the face. "Don't hit me anymore," Oswald pleaded.[3]

As they dragged him to the center aisle, Oswald began hollering, "Police brutality! I haven't done anything!" He also complained that the handcuffs were too tight. Needless to say, since he was accused of killing one officer and had just tried to shoot another, the police had little sympathy for their prisoner. An officer did, however, check the handcuffs. "I reached back and felt that I could get my middle finger in between his wrists and the handcuffs, and in my opinion, they were not too tight," said Officer Bentley.

A large crowd had gathered in front of the building, driven there by rumors that the president's killer was inside. As the police left the building, the crowd surged forward, screaming "Let us have him. We'll kill him! We want him!" The officers formed a wedge with one officer at the point, two immediately on each side of the prisoner, and two behind him. According to Officer Hill, his first thought at that point was, "Here we have just risked our lives to try to catch him; now were going to have to shoot somebody to keep him!" As they pushed their way to the police car, the officers in front pointed their shotguns at the crowd to keep them at bay.[4]

They placed Oswald in the rear seat of an unmarked, four-door, green Ford between officers Paul Bentley and K. K. Lyons. As they made their way to the station, Bentley turned to Oswald and said, "All right. What's your name?" Oswald remained silent.

"Why don't you see if he has any identification?" Hill asked Bentley, who proceeded to take a wallet out of Oswald's left rear pocket. As the police searched for identification, Oswald protested. "I don't know why you are treating me like this. The only thing I have done is carry a pistol in a movie." He continued the protest: "What is this all about? I know my rights." One of the policeman told Oswald that he had done more than just bring a pistol to a movie. "You have killed a policeman." Oswald seemed surprised. "Police officer been killed?" he said innocently. After a few seconds of silence Oswald added: "I hear they burn for murder." Officer Walker replied, "You might find out." The suspect responded calmly, "Well, they say it just takes a second to die."[5]

By now Bentley had rifled through the contents of the wallet and found two identification cards. "Are you Lee Harvey Oswald? That's what this card says. Is that your name?" No answer. Bentley looked at another card. "Hey, this one's got a different name. It looks like Hidell. Alek J. Hidell." He then spelled out the last name: "H-I-D-E-L-L. Same picture, though." Bentley asked which name was real, but Oswald remained silent. "I guess we are going to have to wait until we get to the station to find out who he actually is," someone remarked. [6]

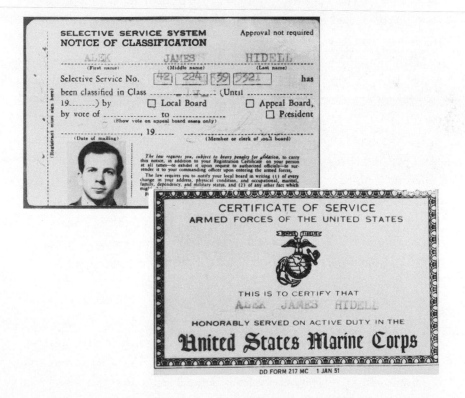

The officers suspected that Oswald may also have been involved in the assassination of President Kennedy. Bentley turned to Oswald and asked: "Did you shoot President Kennedy?" Oswald responded: "You find out for yourself." It would have been the first time that Oswald learned that police had already connected him to the assassination. He showed no emotion — he did not appear shocked or surprised and he offered no objection. They rode the rest of the way in silence.[7]

• • •

Police apprehended Oswald at the Texas Theatre at the same time that LBJ arrived back at Love Field and boarded *Air Force One*. Johnson's top priority was to make arrangements to take the oath of office. At 1:56 p.m., he called Attorney General Robert Kennedy. After offering his condolences, Johnson came to the point of the call: He wanted to know about the oath. Kennedy informed him that anyone could administer the oath. Johnson contacted a local judge, Sarah Hughes, and waited for her to make her way to the plane.

In the meantime, LBJ and his aides contacted the Justice Department to get the exact wording of the presidential oath. In the background they could hear the noise as the *Air Force One* staff removed seats in the back of the plane to make room for the presidential coffin. Johnson kept one eye on the television to keep up with the Dallas investigation. There was a broadcast that the police had entered a theater and arrested a man for killing a Dallas police officer. A few minutes later came a report that the man in custody also worked as a stockman in the Texas School Book Depository. He was the only employee who was missing in the roll call that was taken thirty minutes after the assassination.[8] Oswald was now the leading suspect in the assassination of the president and the murder of a police officer.

• • •

As the police escorted Oswald back to the police station, another drama was playing out at Parkland Hospital where local officials were trying to prevent the Secret Service from removing the president's body. At

1:40 p.m., the president's body was loaded into the casket and ready for transport back to Washington. As they were waiting for the death certificate, a "very pale and agitated" Dr. Earl Rose, the Dallas medical examiner, approached Secret Service agent Roy Kellerman. "There has been a homicide here," he said. "You won't be able to remove the body. We will take it down to the mortuary for an autopsy."[9]

Kellerman, who had just watched his president assassinated, was not about to leave Kennedy's body behind. "My friend, I'm the special agent in charge of the White House detail of the Secret Service. This is the body of the president of the United States and we are going to take it back to Washington." Rose held his ground. "No, that's not the way things are. You're not taking the body anywhere." Kellerman was not impressed. "Doc," he said dismissively, "you are going to have to come up with something a little stronger than yourself to give me the law that this body can't be moved."[10]

The coroner went in search of a judge to provide some legal support, and returned with a local justice of the peace. "It's just another homicide case as far as I'm concerned," he said. The president's men had heard enough at that point. They devised a plan to force their way out of the hospital. With a small army of heavily armed Secret Service agents, they possessed the firepower to do so. With the Secret Service leading the way, they forced their way past a big Dallas cop, loaded the body into the back of an ambulance and raced to Love Field.

•••

At 1:58 p.m., the car carrying Oswald arrived in the basement garage of City Hall. Officially called the "municipal building," it housed the entire Dallas Police Department, the jail, and city courts. It was connected to a newer building that housed city offices and the city Council chambers. Reporters had already started gathering in the basement and on the third-floor police headquarters in anticipation of Oswald's arrival. Gerald Hill told Oswald that they could cover his head if he did not want to be seen and photographed. "We can hold you so that they can't get a picture, if you want. Also, you don't have to answer any of these guys if you don't want to," he said. "Why should I hide my face," Oswald responded, "I haven't done anything to be ashamed of."[11]

They marched him through the garage, past the door, and onto the elevator for the ride to the third floor. As he walked past, reporters got their first glimpse of the man who was the leading suspect in the assassination. Oswald was wearing black slacks, black loafers, a white undershirt and an olive plaid sport shirt, unbuttoned. His left eye was slightly blackened, and there was a cut on his right cheekbone. "Did you shoot the president?" Perhaps noticing the black eye, they asked, "Have you been mistreated by the police." Oswald said nothing.[12]

They got off on the third floor. A small press office, equipped with three old wooden desks and a few battered typewriters, sat at the bottom of the cross-shaped floor. Moving up the green floor on the right side were the Juvenile and Forgery Bureau and a transcribing room. On the left side were signs saying: "Auto Theft," "Burglary and Theft" and, finally, room 317, "Homicide and Robbery." There was a private elevator next to the homicide room that took prisoners to the fifth-floor jail. The rooms occupied by police officials — the chief and assistant chiefs — stood at the top of

the cross. In the cross arm were the elevators that led to the basement, restrooms, and various vending machines for soda, coffee, and cigarettes.[13]

Oswald came off the elevator and walked the twenty feet to the Homicide bureau. The department had two small interrogation rooms where suspects were questioned following their arrest and before being placed in the city jail, and Oswald was placed in the larger of the two. His fourteen-by-ten-foot interrogation room was lined with glass windows that looked out onto other parts of the homicide offices. Inside the room stood a square wooden table and six straight-backed metal chairs. [14]

The detectives initially began interrogating Oswald for the Tippit shooting not realizing that he was also a suspect in the assassination. Gus Rose, who had been busy interviewing witnesses to the Kennedy shooting, asked him his name. Oswald refused to answer. Realizing that Oswald had two forms of identification, one for Lee Oswald, the other for Alek Hidell,

Rose asked: "Which one of these are you?" Oswald gave him a "strange" look and said, "Well, you're the cop, you figure it out!"

Detective James Leavelle entered the room and started questioning the suspect. Oswald was not acting like a man who had just been arrested for shooting a police officer. "He seemed really quite calm, much calmer than I think I would have been under the circumstances had I done what he had done," Leavelle recalled. When he asked Oswald about shooting Tippit, he responded, "I didn't shoot anybody!" Leavelle replied, "Well, you strike me as a relatively intelligent man. You know that we can take that pistol that you had on you and run a ballistics test and prove that your gun was the one used to shoot him." Oswald was not impressed. "Well, you'll just have to do that."[15]

•••

According to the official Secret Service log, the presidential party arrived at Love Field at 2:14 p.m., just as the formal interrogation of Lee Harvey Oswald was about to begin.

CHAPTER 5:

"... *There He Sits*"

Dallas Police Captain J. W. "Will" Fritz, who headed the homicide and robbery bureau, served as Oswald's chief interrogator from the afternoon of November 22 through the morning of November 24, 1963. During that nearly forty-eight-hour period, Fritz questioned Oswald four times, totaling almost twelve hours.[1]

Fritz, who had once helped track down notorious gangsters Bonnie and Clyde, headed every Dallas homicide investigation for the previous thirty years. Born in Texas sometime around the turn of the century (no one knew his exact age), he grew up riding horses and trading mules. In 1920 he traveled to Dallas to realize his ambition of being a police officer. Fritz always wore a distinctive white cowboy hat. His detectives, out of respect for their boss, mimicked his style. Fritz was also a real gun enthusiast. He usually carried three: a .45 automatic clipped to his belt, along with a .32 automatic and a .38 Smith & Wesson that he kept hidden on various parts of his body.[2]

Fritz had devoted his life to police work. Rarely taking days off, he seemed to have no interests outside of work. He lived alone in a hotel room across the street from the police station. He typically spurned small talk, always preferring to keep conversations focused on work. Most of the men who worked with him every day for years knew nothing about him. They did not know whether he was married, single, widowed, or divorced. They respected him and feared him, but few liked him. He was cold, impersonal, and distant. One of his officers described him as unfailingly honest, but also "a hard man and unforgiving man."[3]

Fritz had been assigned to help with security at the Trade Mart on the afternoon of the assassination. When the police chief told him of the shooting he rushed first to Parkland Hospital and then to the book depository building. He arrived at 12:58 p.m. — about twenty-eight minutes after the shooting. Told that the shooter was still in the building, Fritz grabbed a shotgun and started searching inside. While searching the building he was summoned to the sixth floor and the sniper's nest. A few minutes later he was told detectives had found the rifle.

While Fritz was examining the rifle, the building manager approached and informed him that Oswald was missing. Fritz asked for his address and then, accompanied by two officers, drove to the police station to see if Oswald had a criminal record. From there he planned to go to Oswald's place in Irving. At this point, he did not know about the Tippit murder or that Oswald had already been apprehended. [4]

According to Officer Hill, when Fritz arrived at the third-floor police headquarters he instructed the officers to get a search warrant for an address in Irving and bring in a man named Lee Oswald. Hill asked the Captain why he wanted him, and Fritz responded: "He was employed in the book depository and was there just before the shooting but had gone after the shooting and was therefore a suspect." Hill retorted, "Captain, you don't have to go to Irving to get him because there he sits."[5]

•••

Detectives moved Oswald from the small interrogation room into Captain Fritz's office. It was a small room with one large desk, some filing cabinets, and straight-backed chairs for suspects to sit. The room had windows on two sides that looked out into the main room. Fritz would close the blinds whenever he was interrogating a suspect. Most of the formal interrogation took place in this office, although when it got too crowded, Fritz would move the group to the room next door.

At 2:25 p.m., just shy of two hours after the shooting, Fritz stepped into the room to begin the interrogation of Lee Harvey Oswald. The suspect was sitting in a straight-backed chair with his hands cuffed behind his back. Officers Elmer Boyd and Richard Sims stood behind him.[6]

Officer Elmo Cunningham claimed that Fritz was "beyond any question of doubt, the greatest interrogator I've ever heard talk to a person." He placed suspects at ease with a grandfatherly manner, yet he possessed a razor-sharp memory. His strategy was always to ask the same question in many different ways, hoping that the guilty suspect would eventually trip over the details. He was also a careful observer of body language. Fritz's eyes never strayed far from the face of his suspect. "He looked him right in the eye and right in the face the whole time he talked to them so that he noticed the least little quiver of a lip and raising or lowering of the eyelid," recalled Cunningham. Fritz refused to take notes, fearing that it would be distracting and prevent him from establishing an easy rapport with the suspect.

Fritz's goal in any interrogation was to get a signed confession from the suspect. An oral confession was not admissible in Texas court at the time unless it revealed new evidence. Fritz would have to get Oswald to admit to the crime and then to sign an affidavit attesting to his guilt.[7]

Fritz always said that he could get a confession if the suspect had a background similar to his own, ideally someone who was raised on a ranch and who had been around horses. He could understand them and how they thought. He was adept at getting inside their heads and forging a bond that would eventually produce a confession. The man sitting in front of him, however, was like no suspect that he had ever interviewed before.[8]

Staring at his subject through a pair of thick-lensed glasses, Fritz began, as he often did, by trying to establish a rapport. He avoided asking direct questions about the crime. Instead, he eased into the conversation. In his slow, calm voice he initiated the interrogation:

"What is your name, son?"

"You know my name — you got it on my papers you took from me."

"Well, why don't you tell us yourself now just for the record?"

"Lee Harvey Oswald."

"Is that your full name?"

"Yes it is."

"Where do you live?"

"At 1026 Beckley."

"North or South?"

"I don't know."

Fritz was able to determine from Oswald's description of the neighborhood that it was North.[9]

"We found a card in your billfold made out to an Alek J. Hidell. Is that an alias or something?"

Oswald said it was a name he "picked up in New Orleans."[10]

Although initially cooperative, after a few minutes Oswald started complaining. "I think I'm being treated very unfairly here today," he protested. "I got a bad cut over my eye where that policeman hit me, and I don't like having my hands pinned behind my back this way." Fritz, perhaps trying to put the suspect at ease, told the officers to reapply the cuffs so that Oswald's hands could rest in front of his body.

Fritz wanted to go back and ask Oswald more about his address. He was confused. The manager at the book depository had given him Ruth Paine's address for Oswald's residence. But the suspect just told him that he lived in Oak Cliff. Oswald explained that he and his wife were living apart. "I thought it was kind of an awkward arrangement," Fritz told the Warren Commission, so he probed deeper. "I asked him why he didn't stay out there." According to Fritz, Oswald said "he didn't want to stay out there all the time, Mrs. Paine and her husband didn't get along too well."

Realizing that Oswald was living at a different address, Fritz stepped out of the interrogation room and instructed a couple of officers to go to the boarding house and look for evidence. It was a reminder that Fritz was not only the lead interrogator, but also the homicide division supervisor with twenty men under his command and two high-profile murders to solve. In addition to questioning Oswald, Fritz needed to give assignments to officers, listen to reports, find witnesses, and make arrangements for lineups. The added duties prevented him from establishing a sustained conversation with Oswald. At the same time, other law enforcement agencies — namely, the FBI and Secret Service — insisted on getting time with his suspect. "I think it would have been more apt to get a confession out of him or get more true facts from him if I could have got him to sit down and quietly talked with him," Fritz told the Warren Commission.

...

While Fritz interrogated Oswald, Lyndon Johnson took the oath of office on board *Air Force One*. At 2:40 p.m., a little more than two hours after the first shots were fired, Judge Sarah Hughes, her voice shaking and her hands trembling, asked Johnson to recite the oath. Malcolm Kilduff held a dictating machine to record the sound. "Hold up your right hand and repeat after me," the judge said, holding out a Roman Catholic missal that had been retrieved from the president's bedroom. Johnson placed his left hand on the missal, slowly raised his right hand into the air, and recited the thirty-four-word oath. "I do solemnly swear I will faithfully execute the office of president of the United States . . ." In a firm voice Johnson repeated after the judge, ". . . and will to the best of my ability, preserve, protect and defend the Constitution of the United States. So help me God."

Air Force One lifted off at 2:46 p.m., just eight minutes after Lyndon Johnson completed the oath, and 136 minutes after Kennedy had been shot. For the first time, the plane would be carrying two American presidents.

CHAPTER 6:
"Squirming Like a Snared Rat"

During his initial interrogation session with Captain Fritz, Oswald seemed relaxed, cooperative, and confident. His tone and demeanor changed dramatically when FBI agent James P. Hosty Jr. entered the room at 3:15 p.m. It turned out that the two men had a history.

On October 3, the New Orleans office of the FBI asked Hosty, a stocky thirty-five-year-old Notre Dame graduate, to locate Lee and Marina Oswald. Hosty was part of a four-man counterintelligence unit in the Dallas office. He spent most of his time tracking down Klan members and followers of former general Edwin Walker. Considering both Lee and Marina espionage threats, Hosty located Marina at the home of Ruth Paine.

On Friday, November 1, Hosty went to the house to find Oswald. Ruth told him that Lee was not living there and that he was renting at a rooming house in Dallas. She did not know the address but she did tell him that he worked at the book depository building. While they were talking Marina walked into the room. She was frightened that the FBI had come looking for her, but Hosty put her at ease, reassuring her that he was not there to harass her. He asked questions about Lee, and his involvement in the Fair Play for Cuba Committee in New Orleans. Lee was expected home shortly, and they invited Hosty to stay, but he returned to the office. Before leaving, he wrote out his name, office address, and telephone number, and asked Ruth to give it to Lee. Hosty, along with another agent, returned on Tuesday morning, November 5. Once again, however, Oswald was not at home.[1]

On the morning of November 22, Hosty had watched as the presidential limousine drove down Main Street at about ten miles an hour. He was shocked to see how poorly the president was protected. Kennedy rode in an open convertible with no Secret Service agents or police near him. "Why the hell did they station the Secret Service on the vehicle behind him?" he thought. After getting a glimpse of the president he walked over to the Oriental Café for lunch. As a practicing Roman Catholic who declined to eat meat on Friday, Hosty ordered a cheese sandwich with coffee. A few minutes later someone screamed, "They've shot the president!"[2]

At 2:15 p.m., Hosty learned that the police had arrested a man named Lee Oswald for the shooting of a Dallas police officer, and he instantly recalled Oswald's name. He raced back to FBI headquarters and searched through Oswald's file where he found a one-page communiqué from Washington that summarized a letter Oswald had written to the Soviet embassy in Washington. The letter indicated that Oswald had traveled to Mexico City between September 27 and October 2, 1963, where he met with a KGB colonel.

Hosty understood the implications of the communiqué: "If Oswald was in fact Kennedy's killer, then this letter had all the ingredients for a potentially explosive international situation." Were the Soviets behind the assassination? FBI headquarters ordered Hosty to get to police headquarters and interrogate Oswald.[3]

Hosty drove the few blocks to the police headquarters where Oswald was being held. A group from ABC News had commandeered the elevator, trying to squeeze their bulky camera into the narrow space, so Hosty took the stairs. When he arrived on the third floor he was shocked by the chaos. Dozens of reporters, camera crews, and various unidentified people had crammed into the narrow hallways outside Captain Fritz's office. There were huge studio television cameras in the hallway and reporters were broadcasting live. There were blinding flash bulbs going off everywhere. There was so much noise people had to shout to be heard. "Despite the desperate gravity of the situation, police security of the building was obviously extremely lax," he recalled.[4]

Hosty spotted fellow FBI agent James Bookhout, who served as the agency's liaison with the police department's homicide division, standing outside Fritz's office. He pushed his way through the mob of reporters to reach Bookhout, who grabbed Hosty and pulled him into a small outer office next to the interrogation room. "Let's go in," Bookhout said, as he opened the door from Fritz's office and led Hosty inside. There seated in front of him was Lee Harvey Oswald.[5]

• • •

As he entered the room, Hosty spotted a pad of police forms, grabbed it, took out his pen, glanced at his watch, and recorded the time: It was 3:15 p.m. He nodded to Captain Fritz and then looked over at the prisoner. "My first impression of him was that he was a young punk," Hosty recalled in his memoir. "He was sitting there with a wise-ass smirk, the kind you wanted to slap off his face as his deep blue eyes, glaring and beady, confronted you eyeball to eyeball." Hosty described Oswald as "skinny and small, and even though he was only twenty-four years old, he was already losing his hair — his hairline had deeply receded." He noted that Oswald was sporting a "brand-new shiner, still red and slightly swollen, above his right eyebrow."

Hosty introduced himself and told Oswald about his rights. "Special Agent Jim Hosty, with the FBI. I'm here to participate in the interview with the police. I want to advise you of some things. You have the right to remain silent. Anything you say may be used against you in court. You also have the right to have an attorney . . ."

Before he could finish, Oswald interrupted him. "His face had turned ugly," Hosty recalled, "and his whole body jerked in my direction, as if touched by a hot wire." Oswald jumped up and slammed his handcuffed fists on the table. "Oh, so you're Hosty, the agent who's been harassing my wife!" The officers in the room exchanged puzzled looks. What was Oswald's connection to the FBI? Angrily, Oswald continued: "My wife is a Russian citizen who is here in this country legally and is protected under diplomatic laws from harassment by you or any other FBI agent. The FBI is no better than the Gestapo of Nazi Germany." According to Hosty, Oswald was "squirming like a snared rat."[6]

Fritz, fearing he was losing control of the interview, tried to get Oswald to calm down. "I noticed if I talked to him in a calm, easy manner it wasn't very hard to get him to settle down," Fritz recalled. He asked Oswald what he meant when he accused the FBI of accosting his wife. "I thought maybe he meant some physical abuse." Oswald responded: "Well, he threatened her. . . . He practically told her she would have to go back to Russia. . . . He accosted her on two different occasions." After the outburst, Oswald settled down.

Now that Oswald was back under control, Fritz returned to the interrogation, probing deeper, asking more pointed questions directly relevant to the investigation. As Fritz asked questions, Hosty furiously scribbled notes on the pad of police affidavit forms. He later recreated the interrogation in his memoirs.[7]

"Okay now, Lee, you work at the Texas School Depository, isn't that right?"

A polite Oswald responded, "Yeah, that's right."

"When did you start working there?"

"About October 15."

"What did you do down there?"

"I was just a common laborer."

"Now, did you have access to all the floors in that building?"

"Of course."

"Tell me what was on each of those floors."

"The first and second floors have offices. The third and fourth are storage. So were the fifth and sixth."

"And you were working there today, is that right?"

"Yep."

"Were you there when the president's motorcade went by?"

"Yeah."

"Where were you when the president went by the book depository?"

"I was eating my lunch in the first floor."

"What time was that?"

"About noon."

"Were you ever on the second floor around the time the president was shot?"

"Well, yeah. I went up there to get a bottle of Coca-Cola from the machine for my lunch."

"But where were you when the president actually passed your building?"

"On the first floor in the lunchroom."

"And you left the book depository, isn't that right?"

"Yeah."

"When did you leave?"

"Shortly after I heard that the president was shot."

"Why did you leave?"

"Well, I figured with all the confusion there wouldn't be any more work to do that day."

"So what did you do?"

"I took the bus and went home, changed my clothes, and went to a movie."

"Were you carrying a pistol on you when you went to the movie?"

"Yeah."

"Why?"

"'Cause I felt like it."

"Because you felt like it?"

"Yeah, cause I felt like it."

Now, when the police officers apprehended you, did you pull out this pistol?"

"Yeah. I admit I tried to fight the officers at first. I pulled out my gun, but an officer grabbed it and hit me above the eye. I guess I had it coming."

"Do you have a rifle at work?"

"No, I didn't, but the manager of the book depository, Mr. Truly, did."

"How do you know this?"

"Cause he showed it to a bunch of us workers one day on the first floor."

"Do you own a rifle?"

"No, I don't."

"Did you ever?"

"No."

"Have you ever received any firearms training?"

"Well, yeah, in the Marines."

"What level of expertise did you achieve?"

"Marksman."

"Lee, did you shoot the president?"

"No. I emphatically deny that."

"What about the officer in Oak Cliff. Did you shoot him?"

"No. I deny that, too."

Realizing that he was not going to get an easy confession from Oswald, Fritz switched gears. He picked up a folded piece of paper that had been found in Oswald's wallet. It was from "Fair Play for Cuba." He asked: "Now, what's this, Lee?"

Oswald looked over at Hosty and said: "Why don't you ask agent Hosty?" The FBI agent refused to take the bait. He indicated to Fritz that he should continue with his line of questioning.

"You said you have a wife who was a Russian?"

"That's right."

Fritz, clearly unaware of Oswald's past, asked if he had ever been to Russia. "Yes," Oswald replied, "my wife has relatives over there, and she and I still have many friends there."

"How long were you in Russia?"

"About three years."

"What did you do there?"

"Why don't you ask Hosty? He can probably tell you everything you want to know about me."

Fritz looked over to Hosty to see if he wanted to add anything to the discussion. Hosty stopped taking notes for a second. "Captain, I can explain all of this later. Why don't you just continue?"

Fritz, however, appeared agitated. He was getting nowhere with the smooth-talking suspect in front of him, and complicating matters, he had two FBI agents in the room who were preventing him from having the type of one-on-one interaction he preferred with suspects. Perhaps sensing the tension between Oswald and Hosty, Fritz decided to invite Hosty to ask questions.

The FBI agent was worried that Oswald might be a Soviet spy, and that his possible assassination of the president had broader global significance. In his mind, Oswald's trip to Mexico City was key to understanding whether he was acting alone or as part of a larger conspiracy.

Deferring to Fritz, Hosty said: "Ask him if he has ever been in Mexico City."

"Tell us about that, Lee," Fritz said.

"Sure. Sure, I've been to Mexico. When I was stationed in San Diego with the Marines, a couple of my buddies and I would occasionally drive down to Tijuana over a weekend."

Hosty, clearly impatient and dissatisfied with the answer, but also reluctant to impose on Fritz's interrogation, refused to speak directly to Oswald. Instead he instructed Fritz to follow up. "No, not Tijuana. Mexico City. Captain, ask have you ever been to Mexico City."

The question seemed to strike a nerve with Oswald, who started sweating. "What makes you think I've been to Mexico City? I'd never been there. I deny that."

Finally, Hosty felt they were making some progress penetrating Oswald's cocky veneer. "It was clear to me that the Mexico City information was pivotal, and could be Oswald's Achilles' heel," he reflected. "If I just could have gone further with Oswald." Before he could push any further, however, the door swung open and a detective stuck his head in the room to tell Captain Fritz they were ready for a lineup. With that, Fritz stood up and said, "Okay, let's take a break and go do this lineup."

Hosty looked at his watch and jotted down the time in his notes. It was 4:05 p.m.

CHAPTER 7:

"I Don't Care to Answer Any More Questions"

FBI agent James Hosty was not the only person worried that Oswald was part of a larger conspiracy. While Hosty was interrogating the suspect, everyone was beginning to learn of Oswald's unorthodox background. At 3:26 p.m., NBC reported that Oswald had once applied for Russian citizenship. Officials in Washington were discovering the same troubling information.

As soon as he learned that Oswald had been captured and was believed to be the possible assassin, Undersecretary of State George Ball had his name checked against State Department files to see if they had any information on him. They had plenty. "Within minutes," he recalled, "word came back that he had spent thirty-two months in the Soviet Union as recently as June 1962." They quickly discovered that not only had he lived in Moscow, he had also applied for Soviet citizenship. Soon afterwards, they learned that he was involved in a pro-Castro group called Fair Play For Cuba.[1]

The details of Oswald's profile shocked Ball. Everyone assumed that the right wing presented the greatest threat to Kennedy's safety in Dallas. But a communist, and one who once lived in the Soviet Union? The information set off alarm bells at the State Department. Ball called in two experienced Soviet experts, Ambassador Llewellyn Thompson and Averell Harriman. "Could this be a Soviet move to be followed up by a missile attack?" he asked. As Ball recalled, their answer "was a resounding negative." Soviet leaders were too rational to sanction the assassination of an American president. Even if Oswald was not part of an organized plot, Ball worried that his "pretense to Marxist convictions might set off violent anti-Soviet sentiments that could undo all our efforts to develop working arrangements with Moscow." Ball passed the information on to National Security Advisor McGeorge Bundy, who sent it along to *Air Force One*.[2]

The potential Soviet and Cuban connections were especially worrisome. The problem was that if Oswald was acting on orders from either Moscow or Havana, that might make the death of the president potentially part of a global communist offensive. In these early hours that fear still existed, but it was lessening. There were no indications of an international plot. "I had several calls to Washington," recalled Major General Chester Clifton, the president's military advisor on *Air Force One*. "I talked to Bundy himself. It seemed that there were no indications of trouble around the world. He told me that defense was taking its own steps — that defense secretary Robert McNamara was in full charge there."[3]

• • •

In Dallas, Secret Service agent Forrest Sorrels, the head of the Dallas office, had been waiting patiently outside the office while Fritz was conducting the interrogation. Sorrels had joined the Secret Service in 1935 and had once accompanied President Franklin Roosevelt when he spoke at the Cotton Bowl in 1936. He had been nervous about JFK's trip since he learned about it in October. Driving the parade route a few days before the presidential visit, Sorrels cringed as they approached downtown, with its skyscrapers and open windows. "We'd be sitting ducks," he told a colleague. "Any sniper could hit us." [4]

On the day of the visit, Sorrels was in the lead car. After the shooting he traveled to Parkland Hospital and helped escort the president's body back to *Air Force One*. He then drove to the book depository to inspect the crime scene. Once he learned that Oswald was in custody he went to the police station to participate in the interrogation.

At 4:05 p.m., when Fritz opened the door, Sorrels asked if he could question Oswald. "I would like to talk to this man when there is an opportunity," he mentioned. Fritz responded, "You can talk to him right now."[5]

Hosty described Sorrels as "a beaten man." He was in shock. "His hair was mussed, his shoulders drooping. Anguish was etched on his face." Fritz directed the detectives to move Oswald into the other interrogation room for the interview. When Sorrels stepped into the room with a few other agents, Oswald bristled, "I don't know who you fellows are, a bunch of cops?" Sorrels responded, "Well, I will tell you who I am. My name is Sorrels and I am with the United States Secret Service, and here is my commission book." He opened it in front of Oswald, but the suspect did not want to look. He held his head up and stared at the ceiling in defiance. "What am I going to be charged with?" he protested. "Why am I being held? Isn't someone supposed to tell me what my rights are?"[6]

Sorrels informed Oswald that he had the same rights as any other American citizen. He did not have to make a statement, and he had a right to an attorney. Oswald responded: "Aren't you supposed to get me an attorney?" The Secret Service agent tried to break the ice by saying that if he got him an attorney people would say that he was trying to make money off the deal. "You can have the telephone book and you can call anybody you want to," Sorrels explained. He then said, "I just want to ask you some questions. I am in on this investigation. I just want to ask you some questions." Nothing more was said about an attorney. [7]

Sorrels began asking many of the same questions that Fritz had already covered. Where did he work? Where did he live? Why was he living apart from his wife? He asked about his duties at the book depository and whether he had traveled abroad. Oswald patiently responded to all the questions. And then he simply stopped answering. "I don't care to answer any more questions," he said.

Sorrels was surprised by Oswald's casual demeanor. "He was calm," Sorrels told author William Manchester in 1964. "I kept watching his Adam's apple. Usually a telltale sign, but it never bobbed."[8]

The entire conversation lasted about five minutes before Oswald was led from the room to the first lineup.[9]

• • •

Shortly after 4:00 p.m. a group of officers, accompanied by Assistant District Attorney Bill Alexander and Justice of the Peace David Johnston, arrived at Oswald's North Beckley rooming house. "We're police officers. May we come in?" they asked housekeeper Earlene Roberts. They wanted to know if she had a roomer named Lee Harvey Oswald. The housekeeper walked over to a small table, flipped through the registration book.

"No, I don't think we've ever had anyone named Oswald. Who is he?"[10]

"He's a suspect in the assassination. We want to question him. Maybe he's living here under the name of Hidell. Do you have a roomer named Alek Hidell?"

"Hidell? No. I don't recognize that name either. It couldn't be any of our roomers — nobody here would do such a terrible thing."

As she spoke a newsflash came on the television that had been left on in the background. "We take you to the Dallas police station for the first pictures of Lee Harvey Oswald, the man suspected of assassinating President Kennedy," came the announcement. With Oswald's image flashing on the screen, Roberts recognized him. "That man lives here!" She told the officers. "He told us his name was Lee. O.H. Lee, he's been here several weeks. Why, he was home just this noon!" She reported that he changed his jacket and then left. "Mr. Lee! I can't believe it!"

She then led the police officers down a hall into a small room, no more than five feet across, with a single bed and metal headboard, a small table and lamp, an old blond oak dresser with most of the handles missing. Clothes were spilling out of two open drawers. When Alexander opened the closet door he found a brown leather holster hanging from a knob.

Alexander picked up a folded map lying on top of Oswald's dresser, and he spread it out on the bed. It was a map of Dallas with a circle around the downtown area. Inside the circle were several X marks in ink. Alexander immediately saw conspiracy. "That penciled circle approximates the route of the motorcade," he announced to the other officers. One of the X's marked the corner of Elm and Houston from where the shots came. "This is damned significant! It shows premeditation. We can use it in court to prove he planned the assassination!" He also had a theory about the other X marks on the map. "Those might show the

site of another assassin — in case the first one missed. This could be the master map for conspiracy!"

Next to Oswald's bed they also found a pile of books and papers, including copies of the *Daily Worker* and other communist literature. "I think we've got a genuine God damned card-carrying communist on our hands!" Alexander said. "The president might have been the first one on the list," exclaimed a nearly hysterical Johnston. "They might be planning to get some more — undermine the whole country!"

• • •

At roughly the same time, television viewers were getting their first detailed reports about Oswald. NBC reported that Oswald had defected to the Soviet Union in 1959 after service in the Marine Corps. He had lived in Minsk, where he married a Russian woman. In 1962, having grown disillusioned with life in the Soviet Union, he announced that he planned to return to the United States, and the government issued Lee and his wife a passport to enable their return. "He is only a suspect, but he is identified as a prime suspect in the assassination of President Kennedy," NBC announced.

...

Oswald's background had many in Washington worried, including Robert Kennedy. For the previous two years he and his brother had been waging a clandestine guerrilla war against Fidel Castro. When Robert Kennedy heard the first bulletins from Dallas linking Lee Harvey Oswald to pro-Castro activities in New Orleans, he called Enrique "Harry" Ruiz-Williams. Ruiz-Williams was a leader of a group of exiled freedom fighters who were planning raids from guerrilla bases in Central America. "One of your guys did it," Kennedy said to him.[11]

RFK was not accusing Ruiz-Williams of being involved in his brother's death; he was a close friend and a trusted ally. In those initial hours, however, Kennedy was convinced that his enemies — the mafia? pro-Castro elements? disgruntled anti-Castro factions? — were behind the assassination. He even confronted the head of the CIA, asking him directly if his agency had been behind the shooting. Police officials in Dallas, and the FBI in Washington, were moving toward the conclusion that Lee Harvey Oswald was the lone assassin, but RFK remained skeptical. In the months and years that followed, he would launch his own private investigation into his brother's death, driven by the belief that, if he was guilty at all, Oswald was only the tip of the iceberg.

Robert Kennedy was not alone in his private quest to uncover the truth about the assassination. Hundreds of miles away, in Havana, Cuba, Fidel Castro was engaging in a similar exercise. "Fidel very quickly became an expert on the assassination," recalled former CIA analyst Brian Latell. "As soon as he heard that it had happened he got on the phone with Cuban intelligence and said 'bring me all the files.'" Castro created a special group in the interior ministry to investigate and track all the information about the assassination.[12]

CHAPTER 8:

"Did You Kill the President?"

Since it was clear that the police were not going to obtain a confession from Oswald, they would need to build the case against him by gathering as much evidence as possible.

At this point police only possessed circumstantial evidence connecting Oswald to the Kennedy assassination — they knew he worked at the book depository building from where the bullets were fired; that he had access to the sixth floor where the sniper's nest had been constructed; and that he had fled the building after the shooting. There was a witness they still needed to bring in who claimed to have seen someone who matched Oswald's description in the sixth-floor window. For the Tippit murder, however, they had multiple witnesses. They needed to get these witness into the station to pick him out of a lineup.

At 4:30 p.m. three detectives escorted Oswald out of the interrogation room and into the hallway for the twenty-foot walk to the elevator that would bring him downstairs for the first of three lineups that day. Oswald would get his first glimpse of the media frenzy his actions had created.

...

It had been standard practice for the Dallas Police Department to cooperate with reporters. Local journalists often accompanied police on patrol and were even asked to assist officers in the line of duty — typing confessions from suspects. In return for their cooperation, reporters received special access and exclusives. "We had a two-way street," recalled Eddie Baker, a local news director, "and we scratched a lot of backs and we had our backs scratched in return." Earlier that year, in February 1963, Chief Jesse Curry had threatened disciplinary action against any officer who violated department policy toward the media.[1]

Within hours of Oswald's arrest more than three hundred representatives of the news media from around the world gathered in Dallas. The Warren Commission concluded that on the evening of November 22 there were more than one hundred reporters on the third-floor of police headquarters. FBI agent Hosty described the scene on the police department's third floor as "not too much unlike Grand Central Station at rush hour, maybe like the Yankee Stadium during the World Series games, quite noisy." James Leavelle later compared the police station to a modern-day Walmart store.[2]

The Dallas police had set up no parameter and lax security around the jail. There were no guards stationed at key entry points into the building. Anyone could have entered the building, taken the elevator to the third floor, and positioned themselves within feet of America's most notorious prisoner since John Wilkes Booth. Technicians ran thick cables through offices, out windows, and down the side of the building. Reporters wandered into offices and freely used police telephones.[3]

Chief Curry, although clearly overwhelmed by the amount of press scrutiny, was determined to maintain his policy of cooperating with the media. He did not want the national reporters who had descended on Dallas to report that Oswald was being abused while he was in police custody. It especially disturbed him to hear a reporter telling a television audience, as he held up a picture of Oswald, that "this is what the man who was charged with shooting President Kennedy looks like, or at least this is what he did look like. We don't know what he looks like now after being in custody of the police." Curry knew Oswald wasn't being mistreated, but the comments, no matter how inaccurate, stung just the same.

The only way he could prove to the world that the Dallas police were not mistreating their infamous prisoner was to allow the media to see him as often as possible. Past practice of cooperating with the media and

Curry's desire to prove that Oswald was not being abused in police custody, led to the frantic and crowded conditions on the third floor of the Dallas police headquarters.[4]

Each time Oswald was escorted from Fritz's office to his jail cell he had to be paraded past dozens of reporters who had gathered at City Hall. "[I]f you ever slopped hogs and throw down a pail of slop and saw them rush after it you would understand what that was like up there," recalled Leavelle.[5]

•••

As Oswald entered the hallway, flashbulbs popped and reporters shouted questions. Oswald seemed to relish the attention, raising his handcuffed fists for the photographers. "Did you kill the president?" a reporter shouted. "No, sir. Nobody charged me with that," Oswald responded calmly. He then disappeared into the elevator for the ride to the basement. [6]

Shockingly, it was not until Oswald arrived downstairs that detectives searched him for the first time. While in the car to the station, officers had removed Oswald's wallet to check for identification, and they had taken his gun. But no one had bothered to search his body to see if he was carrying another concealed weapon. Now, two hours after his arrest, officers Sims and Boyd discovered five .38 shells in his front left pants pocket. Boyd asked him why he was carrying these bullets. "I just had them in my pocket," Oswald responded. Sims also found a bus transfer slip in Oswald's shirt pocket. They recovered a few other items from his pockets, including $13.87. Oswald removed his Marine Corps ring and handed it to Sims.[7]

•••

In a typical lineup a suspect would be handcuffed to three other prisoners and led out onto a stage. Given that many people suspected that Oswald had assassinated the president, Fritz worried about his safety. He did not want to put Oswald in close proximity with other prisoners so he asked three police department employees — two officers and a clerk — to remove their jackets and ties and appear next to Oswald in the lineup.

The decision to use police department personnel would become a source of contention for Oswald and, later, his defenders. Oswald complained bitterly that he was set up, forced to stand in a lineup next to clean cut, well-dressed men while he was disheveled and sporting a black eye.

At 4:35 p.m. the detectives led Oswald into the lineup room. Oswald stood on a raised platform under the number 2. Each man was then asked to step forward and state his age, address, where he went to school, and where he was born. Oswald answered all the questions.

There was no formal partition between the suspects and the witnesses. An emotionally distraught Helen Markham, who had witnessed the Tippit murder, stood a few feet away. Only the bright lights directed at him prevented Oswald from seeing Markham. She requested that the men be instructed to turn sideways, which was the angle she saw the man who shot Tippit. "The second one," she said. Having been positively identified, Oswald returned to the third-floor interrogation room. Fritz now had some hard evidence to work with.[8]

•••

Oswald was once again forced to run the third-floor gauntlet of reporters on his way back to the interrogation room. Fred Kaufman, a photographer for the Associated Press, stood in the hallway holding his camera above the crowd trying to get a picture of the suspect. Behind him he heard someone say "Eddie." It wasn't his name but he turned around and saw a stocky, balding, middle-aged man. "Excuse me. I thought you were Eddie Benedict," a local Dallas photographer. "My name is Jack Ruby," he said. "I own the Carousel Club. This card will entitle you to be my guest at the club any time." Ruby bragged that his club was the only one that had closed for three days in honor of Kennedy's memory. He then disappeared in the crowd.[9]

•••

More evidence was coming back from the field. A group of six detectives, headed by Gus Rose, had descended on Ruth Paine's home. "I've been expecting you to come out," said Paine who sat in the living room

with Marina, who cradled her infant daughter, Rachel, in her arms. "Come right in." While the officers scoured the house, Rose called Fritz to see if there was anything in particular he needed. "Well, ask her if her husband has a rifle," was the response. Ruth translated the question into Russian for Marina who, after initially saying no, quickly recalled that he kept a rifle in the garage.[10]

The detectives led Marina and Ruth out the back door, past the baby clothes hanging on the line, and into the garage, which was too cluttered with boxes to have room for a car. Maria pointed toward an old blanket, rolled up and tied with white twine. Marina was relieved to see the carpet still rolled up on the garage floor, but when one of the officers picked it up, it went limp.[11]

Rose brought the women back into the living room where he called Fritz with this crucial piece of information. Fritz could now establish that Oswald owned a rifle and that it was missing. He told detectives to bring Maria and Ruth Paine to the station. He wanted to see if Marina could positively identify the rifle recovered from the third floor of the book depository building. The other officers continued to search the house and

garage where they found several hundred "Freedom for Cuba" leaflets.

While the police were at the house, Linnie Mae Randall, who had watched Oswald place a mysterious package into her brother's car that morning, approached them. She had been watching television and heard Oswald's name mentioned. She pointed out that her brother was Buell Wesley Frazier, the man who drove Oswald to work that morning. "I saw Lee come to our house and get in the car this morning," she told them. "He was carrying a long package, wrapped in brown paper. I don't know what it was, but it sure did seem funny to me for him to be taking something that big to work." Her brother might be able to shed more light on the subject, she said. The officer wrote down the information in his book and thanked her.[12]

Other detectives were searching for potential witnesses. Using the transfer found on Oswald they tracked down bus driver Cecil McWatters. He recognized his distinctive hole punch in the transfer, confirming that Oswald had boarded his bus and later got off around 1:00 p.m. They also found Ted Callaway and Sam Guinyard, who had seen the gunman fleeing the scene of the Tippit murder. Detectives picked them up and started making arrangements for a second lineup.

• • •

While police in Dallas were assembling a case against Oswald, *Air Force One*, carrying the new president and the body of the slain leader, was approaching Andrews Air Force Base outside Washington. The plane touched down at 5:58 p.m. (Eastern Time).

A coatless and hatless Lyndon Johnson walked down the steps of *Air Force One* as an honor guard presented arms and a military band played "Hail to the Chief." The new president then walked over to a battery of TV cameras and lights. Lyndon Johnson was about to introduce himself to the nation. All the major news networks across the nation carried his arrival and statement. Johnson's Texan drawl must have been surprising to a nation that had grown accustomed to Kennedy's crisp New England accent. "This is a sad time for all people. We have suffered a loss that cannot be weighed. For me, it is a deep personal tragedy. I know the world shares the sorrow that Mrs. Kennedy and her family bear. I will do my best. That is all I can do. I ask for your help — and God's."

CHAPTER 9:

"The Number-Two Man"

At 6:20 p.m., Oswald was once again brought down to the basement, next to the same men and in the same order, and marched out onto the same stage. Ted Callaway and Sam Guinyard, who had seen Oswald running from the scene of the Tippit murder with a gun in his hand, stood a few feet away. Callaway wanted to see the suspects from the same distance that he viewed the shooting of officer Tippit. He got up and walked to the back of the room. When he came back he whispered to one of the officers, "The short one — number two." Guinyard agreed. "That's the one."[1]

After they identified Oswald in the lineup, Callaway and Guinyard were taken to the crime lab on the fourth floor where they were shown a jacket that was found along the route that Oswald took following the Tippit shooting. They identified it as similar to the one they saw Oswald wearing.[2]

Also viewing the lineup was bus driver Cecil J. McWatters, who picked up Oswald shortly after the assassination. He was less certain. "There's one feller up there is about the size and build of the man who got on my bus and then asked for a transfer and got off." The detective asked which one. "The number-two man," McWatters said. "But I couldn't positively identify him. That's just the size and general complexion."[3]

• • •

After the lineup, police escorted Oswald back to the third floor, past the horde of reporters, and placed him back into Fritz's office. As the police gathered more evidence, Oswald became less cooperative. He had now been through two lineups. But who was behind the bright lights? Were they witnesses who had seen him in the sixth-floor window and positively identified him as the president's assassin? Were they witnesses from Officer Tippit's murder? He was uncertain how much evidence the police had assembled. Oswald, in fact, had reason to be nervous because Fritz finally had some evidence to use against his uncooperative suspect.

Oswald began the next interrogation by announcing that he would not continue talking without a lawyer. Fritz explained that he could have a lawyer present at any time. Oswald did not want just any lawyer, however. He demanded that a "Mr. Abt" represent him. "I don't know him personally, but that is the lawyer I want. . . . If I can't get him then I may get the American Civil Liberties Union to get me an attorney." Oswald told Fritz that he did not have money to pay for a call. Fritz informed him that he was allowed to make a collect call from the jail.[4]

Since the 1950s, John Abt had been a prominent civil liberties lawyer who defended communists from government persecution. He participated in high-profile challenges to the Alien Registration Act, which led to the imprisonment of the Communist Party leadership, and the McCarran Internal Security Act, which made Party membership illegal.

By choosing Abt to represent him, Oswald may have revealed a great deal about his defense strategy. Critics eventually claimed that Oswald shot Kennedy because he wanted to be famous, but if that was the case, Oswald would have worn the assassination as a badge of honor. If he wanted the world to know him as the man who shot JFK why would he deny being the assassin? Either Oswald genuinely viewed himself as a victim of a massive government conspiracy or he planned to use his trail as political theater — as a platform to talk about his ideas and to place the government on trial. As a young man, Oswald had been fascinated by Ethel and Julius Rosenberg, who were executed for being Soviet spies. They never admitted their guilt, and they quickly became international celebrities and martyrs.

Denying the charges also gave Oswald something that he desperately needed: control. As long as he refused to cooperate, the police needed him.

Fritz would have to continue spending hours talking with him, trying to solicit information, treating him with a gentleness that would disappear once he admitted the truth.

At 7:04 p.m., Fritz stepped out of the interrogation room to confer with police chief Jesse Curry, Assistant District Attorney William Alexander, and local justice of the peace David Johnston. "How's the case coming?" Curry asked. "We're getting ready to file on him for the shooting of the officer," Fritz replied. "What about the assassination?" Curry asked. "I strongly suspect that he was the assassin of the president," Fritz responded, but he needed more time to gather evidence.

Alexander, who was still shaken by what he had seen in Oswald's room, wanted to file charges as quickly as possible. "Captain Fritz and I had decided to file on him for Tippit, before some communist lawyer tried to get him out on bond," he said later.[5]

At 7:10 p.m., Oswald was moved into an adjacent room and formally charged with the murder of officer Tippit. "I didn't shoot anybody," Oswald protested. When Alexander started reading the charge, Oswald interrupted, "Don't tell me about it. Tell my legal representative." He claimed that he could only be arraigned for murder in the courthouse. "This isn't a court. You can't arraign me in a police station. I can only be arraigned in a courtroom. How do I know this is a judge?" Alexander cut him off. "Shut up and listen," he admonished. "The way you're treating me, I might as well be in Russia," Oswald snapped.[6]

Afterward, Alexander gave a full report of the exchange to reporters. "As a lawyer and officer of the court, I will do everything I can to see that Oswald gets a fair trial. But, as an individual, I detest him. He's the most arrogant person I've ever met. I got the impression he enjoys being in the spotlight. It's obvious he is a communist sympathizer." He claimed that throughout the proceeding Oswald "kept interrupting" to insist "on his constitutional rights." The prisoner "claimed we were mistreating him, but I've never seen a murder suspect handled more considerately. He dished out a lot of verbal abuse, but I didn't see anything to indicate anyone had abused him."[7]

...

Down the hallway, just a few feet from where Lee sat, police questioned Marina. An officer carried the rifle found in the book depository down the hallway and placed it in front of her. Did she recognize the weapon? In Russian, she said that it could be the rifle that her husband owned, but she could not be sure. A detective pointed to the telescopic sight, hoping that she would recognize this distinctive feature. Again, she could not positively identify it.

Marina asked to see her husband, but police told her he could not be disturbed. A few minutes later, she noticed a commotion in the next office. She looked up to see her mother-in-law, Marguerite — a short, round-faced woman wearing black horn-rimmed glasses and a white nurse's uni-form — marching into the room.

When she learned that her son had been implicated in the assassina-tion, Marguerite, for some reason, called the news desk at the *Fort Worth Star-Telegram* and hitched a ride to the Dallas police headquarters with two reporters, including a young Bob Schieffer. On the way to Dallas, Marguerite seemed less concerned about her son's fate than her own future. She complained that Marina would get all the public sympathy and that no one would "remember the mother."

The two embraced, before Marina placed Rachel into Marguerite's arms. "I didn't know I was a grandmother again," she said. "Nobody told me."[8]

The two women had a strained relationship. In July 1962, Lee and Marina had moved in with Marguerite. The arrangement lasted for two weeks and led to a permanent rift between mother and son. It became apparent to Marina that Lee "did not love his mother, she was not quite a normal woman." The mother complained that Marina and Lee spoke Rus-sian around the house and made no effort to include her in conversations. At one point, Marguerite scolded Marina: "You took my son away from me!" Lee, who had stopped speaking to his mom, made arrangements to move out without telling his mother.[9]

Since Marina could not speak English the two women depended on Ruth Paine to translate. Marguerite quickly took control of the room. She interrogated Ruth about why she never called to tell her that she was a grandmother. Ruth, apologetically, said: "Marina wanted to contact you, but Lee didn't want her to." When Marguerite learned that Marina had signed a statement that Lee owned a rifle, she began debating with the police, insisting that her son never owned a gun and that Marina must have misunderstood the question.

Marguerite would become the world's first conspiracy advocate. As Marguerite fought with the police, Lee's older brother Robert walked into the room. She quickly pulled him aside and lectured him that if Lee shot the president he must have been carrying out official government orders. She believed that Lee went to Russia as an American agent, most likely a top spy for the CIA. "Lee could have been involved," she told William Manchester in 1964. "But some other people were too." She would later suggest that her son should be honored for his long years of service to the CIA by being buried at Arlington National Cemetery.[10]

Marguerite had always seen the misfortune in her life as the product of some conspiracy. Robert, who had grown up listening to his mother's paranoid stories, did not want to hear them today. "Oh mother, forget it," Robert scolded her.[11]

Her son was facing the possibility of the electric chair, but Marguerite had other priorities on November 22. Later that evening, she made a deal with reporters from *Life* magazine to give them access to her and Marina in exchange for money. Her son was the most notorious man in the world and Marguerite was determined to cash in on his celebrity status. "I'm sorry for Mrs. Kennedy and Marina but they have money," she said in 1964. "I have nothing."[12]

• • •

By 7:20 p.m., Oswald was back in the interrogation room next to Fritz's office, and there was a new face in the room — FBI agent Manning C. Clements. Arriving at police headquarters shortly after the president's shooting, Clements realized that no one from the agency had questioned Oswald in depth about his background. They did not even have a detailed physical description of the leading suspect.

Fritz allowed Manning to lead the questioning, eliciting from Oswald basic background information — his age, place of birth, height, and weight.

He then asked Oswald about the fake selective service card that was found in his wallet with the name Alek James Hidell.

What was the purpose of this card?, he asked. Oswald remained evasive, refusing to answer the questions directly. After a few minutes, an officer opened the door and said that Oswald was needed downstairs for another lineup.[13]

At 7:28 p.m., Oswald was once again led through the crush of reporters. Flashbulbs popped as reporters hurled questions. As the detective struggled to move the prisoner toward the elevator, Oswald used the occasion to communicate directly to the media, creating a carnival-like atmosphere. "These people here have given me a hearing without legal representation," Oswald, referring to his arraignment, said into a microphone shoved in his direction. "Did you shoot the president?" A reporter asked. "I didn't shoot anybody," Oswald replied. "No, sir."

• • •

The third lineup took place at 7:40 p.m. Oswald was again number two in the lineup. On the other side of the screen were sisters-in-law Barbara and Virginia Davis. As soon as Oswald stepped into the bright lights both Davis women identified him. "That's him," they said, "the second one from the left." He was the man they saw running from the Tippit murder scene.

Also in the room was Howard Brennan. He was a key witness for Fritz since he was the only person who could place Oswald in the sixth-floor window right before the shooting. He had provided police with the initial description that likely led Officer Tippit to confront Oswald. Brennan, however, refused to positively identify Oswald. "He looks like him. But the man I saw wasn't disheveled like this fella," he told police. He later told the Warren Commission that he recognized Oswald as the man in the sixth-floor window with the rifle, but he feared that if there was a conspiracy he would be placing himself and his family in danger by coming forward as a witness.[14]

• • •

As the details of Oswald's background reached Washington they caused confusion at the White House, where the initial assumption had been that a right-winger had killed Kennedy. Now, they were getting reports that Oswald had ties to the left. "No one knows yet who the killer is — whether a crazed Birchite or a crazed Castroite," the historian Arthur Schlesinger wrote in his journal that evening. "I only know that the killer has done an incalculable disservice to this country and to all mankind."[15]

CHAPTER 10:

"I Know the Tactics of the FBI"

At 7:55 p.m., as detectives led Oswald off the elevator and down the hallway to Fritz's office, Oswald told newsmen that the only reason he was in custody was because of his stay in the Soviet Union, defiantly adding, "I'm just a patsy!"

At 8:05 p.m. Oswald settled in his chair in Fritz's office with FBI agent Clements picking up where he left off. He asked Oswald to provide the names, addresses, and occupations of relatives, along with a chronological list of all the places where he had lived and worked. According to another FBI agent in the room at the time, "Oswald just answered the questions as asked to him. He didn't offer any information. He sat there quite stoically, not much of an expression on his face."[1]

Finally, on a perfectly innocuous question about his present occupation, Oswald exploded; "What started out to be a short interrogation turned out to be rather lengthy," he complained. "I refused to be interviewed by other law enforcement officers before and I've got no intention of being interviewed by you. I know the tactics of the FBI. You're using the soft touch. There's a similar agency in the Soviet Union. Their approach would be different, but the tactics would be the same. I believe I've answered all the questions I'm going to answer, I don't care to say anything else."

With that, Oswald stood up as if he were going to just walk out of the room. He quickly sat back in the chair and repeated, "I don't care to talk anymore." Another fruitless interrogation session had come to an end.[2]

• • •

Oswald's angry and unpredictable response only confirmed Fritz's belief that all of these law enforcement people aggravated Oswald, making it more difficult to get a confession. He was convinced that if he could get his suspect alone and just talk with him that, eventually, he would let down his guard and talk about the assassination. At 8:30 p.m., after Clements had left the room, Fritz continued the questioning. A more relaxed Oswald did not hesitate to answer his questions.

"Did you keep a rifle in Mrs. Paine's garage in Irving?"

"No."

"Well, the people out at the Paine residence say you did have a rifle, and you kept it out there wrapped in a blanket."

"That isn't true."

"You know you've killed the president. This is a very serious charge."

"No, I haven't killed the president."

"He is dead."

"Yeah, well, people will forget that in a few days and there will be another president."[3]

• • •

At 8:55 p.m., crime-lab sergeant W. E. "Pete" Barnes entered Fritz's office to make a cast of Oswald's hands and right cheek. The process involved heating paraffin until it formed a waxy paste and then brushing it onto the skin. As the wax cooled it extracted nitrates from the skin, which, theoretically, could reveal whether a gun had been fired. The hardened casts were then removed and sent to a lab. The tests were notoriously unreliable, but still a part of standard police practice in Dallas.

As Barnes unpacked the equipment he explained to Oswald what he was about to do. "I'm going to make a paraffin cast of your hands." As the handcuffs were removed, Oswald asked: "What are you trying to prove? That I fired a gun?" Barnes said that it was up to the lab technicians, not him, to decide whether he had fired a gun.[4]

Oswald patiently endured the procedure, allowing Barnes to paint layers of the glue-like substance on his hands and his cheek, before cutting the paraffin off with scissors. After Barnes removed the casts from Oswald's right cheek and his hands, he carried them down to the evidence room. (The tests proved inconclusive, but that did not stop Dallas police officials from leaking to the press reports that the test proved that Oswald had fired a gun.) A few minutes later he returned to take Oswald's finger- and palm- prints. Oswald remained silent through the entire process, but when Barnes asked him to sign the fingerprint card, he snapped: "I'm not signing anything until I talk to an attorney."[5]

While Barnes was performing the tests Fritz stepped into another office and talked to Buell Wesley Frazier, the man who had driven Oswald to work that morning. Fritz learned for the first time that Oswald had placed a large bag in the backseat of the car that morning, claiming that it was curtain rods. Frazier also mentioned that it was unusual for Oswald to go to Irving on a Thursday evening. For Fritz this was another critical, though circumstantial, piece of evidence. He had Oswald's wife telling him that he kept a rifle at the house. Now he learned that Oswald had made an unexpected visit to the house on Thursday night and carried a large paper bag that could have contained a rifle with him to work that morning.[6]

Fritz walked down the hall to where Marina and Ruth Paine were being held and asked Marina if she could confirm Frazier's story. She said she did not see Lee leave that morning so she could not say whether he carried a package with him or not. But Lee had said nothing to her about needing curtain rods for his room.[7]

• • •

At 9:00 p.m., while Oswald sat in the interrogation room with two police officers standing over him, Fritz met with Bill Alexander, and former assistant district attorney Jim Allen. Alexander was still excited about the map they had recovered from Oswald's room. "That map we found on Beckley is a fine piece of evidence. If we can prove it shows premeditation, it will be the biggest thing we've got going for a death sentence. But I'm worried about something else. All that communist stuff we found — even the map — makes it look like a conspiracy. I'm real suspicious."[8]

The three men decided to get some fresh air so they walked a few blocks to the Majestic steakhouse, a popular place for local law enforcement officials. At the restaurant they met Forrest Sorrels, the head of the Dallas Secret Service office, who was there with two assistants. They all sat at a large table near the back of the restaurant, ordered steaks and coffee, and talked about the day's events.

Fritz laid out the evidence they had against Oswald. They could place him on the sixth floor where they found the empty cartridges, the rifle, and the paper bag. They knew that he left the building shortly after the shooting. His landlady said that he left his apartment at around one o'clock. He admitted that he had a gun when he left the house. They had eyewitnesses who saw him shoot officer Tippit. He was captured in a movie theater carrying a gun. They knew from his wife that he owned a rifle and that it was missing from the garage.

Left unsaid, however, was what they did not have at this point: a witness who could confidently identify Oswald as the shooter in the sixth-floor window, forensic evidence tying Oswald to the rifle, or even proof that the rifle used in the assassination belonged to Oswald. Most of all, they lacked a cooperative suspect.

When asked about the interrogation, Fritz responded: "As long as we talk quietly he's all right, but anytime I ask him an important question he clams up. He seems to anticipate what I'm going to ask. I don't think I'll get a confession anytime soon, if ever. Of course, the conditions are so difficult — all those people, the FBI, reporters. It isn't easy to interrogate under those circumstances."[9]

Alexander was not surprised by Oswald's refusal to cooperate. "I think he's a communist so I doubt if he'll talk," he declared. The district attorney did not think a confession would be necessary to prosecute the case. "It looks to me like we might have a real conspiracy on our hands and I think we need to charge him as soon as we can." He urged Fritz to file charges as quickly as possible, even though the detective had just said he did not have enough evidence against his suspect. "You have to remember," the jittery DA said, "this is an historic case and you ought to try to file on him before midnight to show you got your man and charged him on the same day." Fritz agreed, but made clear that he wanted more evidence before filing. "I'd like to wait until we develop the firearm and fingerprint evidence before proceeding with any charges in the assassination."[10]

•••

When they went back to City Hall after dinner, Alexander ran into his friend, George Carter of the *Times Herald.* "Are you going to file?" Carter asked. Alexander replied that he planned to file a complaint stating that Oswald "did then and there voluntarily and with malice aforethought kill John F. Kennedy by shooting him with a gun in furtherance of a communist conspiracy." Not only was Alexander convinced that Oswald was part of the conspiracy, he also wanted to squelch rumors that Kennedy had been killed by Dallas right-wingers. There had been no mention of Oswald being a part of any conspiracy in any of the interrogation sessions, and no evidence to suggest it. The police had not even developed enough evidence to charge him with shooting Kennedy, let alone being a player in an international assassination plot. [11]

Within minutes the story hit the wires and flashed on television sets across the country. Lyndon Johnson, who was relaxing at home in Washington, was shocked when he saw the flash. He worried about the inflammatory nature of the charges. That was not what the nation needed right now. "We must not start making accusations without evidence," he told aides gathered around his living room. "It could tear this country apart."[12]

LBJ asked his aide Horace Busby to call the attorney general of Texas, Waggoner Carr. "Tell him the country needs the most responsible, the most thorough investigation, and I seem to remember that there is some law in Texas permitting the attorney general to take over in a situation like this." Carr called Chief Curry and had the story retracted.

CHAPTER 11:

"He Is Really a Good Boy"

By Friday evening, millions of Americans gathered around their television sets to see the first glimpse of the man suspected of shooting the
president. Sandwiched between old footage of JFK speeches, updates on
the actions of the new president, and interviews with people on the street,
NBC gave the world its first look at Lee Harvey Oswald.

Within hours of the shooting, an announcer told viewers that Oswald
was being held for the killing of a Dallas police officer, and that he was
considered a prime suspect in the assassination of President Kennedy. NBC
also reported that Oswald "has denied any knowledge of the assassination
of the president." NBC offered fragments of Oswald's unorthodox background: that he had once turned in his American passport to the Soviet
Embassy in Moscow; that he had been arrested in New Orleans for dis-
tributing material for a group called "Fair Play for Cuba;" and that he was
married to a Russian woman. The network played the full interview that
Oswald had given to a local television station in New Orleans. For millions
of Americans it would be the first time they would see Oswald's face and
hear his voice.

As the evening wore on, NBC reported on the evidence police had
collected — the rifle and spent cartridges in the school book depository along
with eyewitnesses who placed Oswald at the scene. They made clear, however, that Oswald continued to insist on his innocence. Reporters in Dallas, mimicking law enforcement officials, described Oswald as "arrogant,"

"defiant," and "stoic." By late evening, NBC showed millions of viewers the images of Oswald being paraded through the narrow hallway on his way back and forth from the police lineups. Viewers also saw images of his wife, mother, and small daughter as they arrived at police headquarters. "I am heartbroken about this," Marguerite told reporters. "He is really a good boy."

• • •

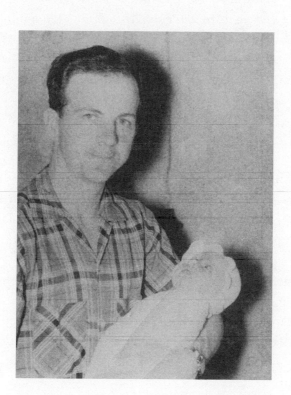

At 11:20 p.m. Chief Curry was pushing Fritz to file charges against Oswald for killing Kennedy. "Have we got enough to charge Oswald with the president's murder?" Curry asked Fritz. They had obtained no new evidence since their last discussion when Fritz said he wanted more time before filing. They were all convinced he was guilty; at this point, they just could not prove it. But they were under pressure to file charges. "We wanted to file on him before midnight," Alexander told author Vincent

Bugliosi. "It just would look better that we got the SOB on the same day he killed Kennedy."[1]

At 11:26 p.m., the Dallas district attorney Alexander, who a few hours earlier had accused Oswald of being part of an international communist conspiracy, drafted the language of the formal charges against Oswald. Fritz and Wade signed it and then passed it on to Judge David Johnston, who added his signature along with the time: "Filed, 11:26 p.m., November 22, 1963." A few hours earlier, Fritz had asked for more time to gather evidence before charging Oswald. He had discovered no new evidence, but he was convinced that Oswald was his man, and the police believed there was important symbolic value in presenting charges on the same calendar day as the assassination.[2]

...

While Fritz, Curry, and Alexander were making plans to charge him, Oswald was sitting in the interrogation room under the supervision of two detectives. Only a few yards away, on the other side of the door to Fritz's office, Jack Ruby stood rubbing shoulders with members of the media.

Earlier in the evening he had gone to his synagogue to pray for the fallen president. After leaving the synagogue, he heard on the radio that the police were working late. Seeing an opportunity to ingratiate himself to the police, Ruby stopped by a local delicatessen, picked up ten corned beef sandwiches with mustard (they only made eight sandwiches by mistake) along with ten soft drinks — eight black cherries and two celery tonics — and brought them to police headquarters.

He arrived at the station a few minutes before 11:00 p.m. Officer Elmo L. Cunningham, who was leaving for the evening, ran into Ruby as he stepped off the elevator on the first floor. "Jack what are you doing down here this time of night?" Cunningham asked. "Oh, just rubbernecking," he replied. "No," he added, "I know some of those guys up there hadn't had a chance to go eat, so I just went out and got a sack of sandwiches to take over here."[3]

This was Ruby's second visit to the third floor of the police station. At no time did anyone attempt to stop him, or ask him for credentials.

After making small talk Ruby positioned himself outside Fritz's office door. He hung around outside the interrogation room offering information to some of the reporters, most of whom were out of town and did not know the main characters. At one point, Ruby reached for the door and started to step into the room were Oswald was being interrogated before being stopped by officers. "You can't go in there, Jack," he was told.[4]

Ike Pappas, a radio reporter for WNEW in New York, had flown to Dallas as soon as he learned that Kennedy had been shot. By early evening he was camped out on the third floor of the police department. He was trying to get an interview with Henry Wade, but a throng of reporters surrounded the district attorney. "I was trying to get to Henry Wade's office and up comes this guy in a black pin-striped suit . . . and a little fedora . . . stubby little guy." He assumed the guy was a vice cop. "'Are you a reporter?" asked the approaching man. Pappas said yes, and then asked if he was a policeman. "No, I'm Jack Ruby," he said. "I run the Carousel Club down the block." He handed Pappas a card and invited him to come by and bring his friends.

Pappas was not interested in Ruby's gentleman's club, but he was trying to get an interview with Wade. "I got your card," he said to Ruby, "now can you get me a telephone?" As Ruby looked around, Pappas said, "I want to talk to Henry Wade, but I need a telephone." "I'll get you a telephone," Ruby said. He walked over to Wade, who was meeting with reporters, and said, "Hey, this guy's from New York. Can he use your phone? And he wants to do an interview." Wade responded: "Yeah, but I'm busy with these reporters. Put him on the phone, and I'll be in in a minute." Ruby then escorted Pappas into Wade's office. A few minutes later, Wade walked in and gave Pappas an interview.[5]

• • •

At Bethesda Naval Hospital outside Washington, D.C., doctors were immersed in the grim work of performing an autopsy while morticians struggled to camouflage the president's head wound. They had expected the process to take a few hours, but doctors were having a hard time figuring out the trajectory of the president's bullet wounds, and the morticians had difficulty reconstructing JFK's shattered head. At the time no decision had been made about whether there would be an open casket, so the morticians aimed for precision.

The long delay gave members of the Kennedy family gathered on the hospital's seventeenth floor plenty of time to reminisce and share stories of happier times. Family and friends now joined the original group that had been in Dallas. Jackie described in graphic detail every aspect of the shooting and the painful minutes that followed. "I was so startled and shocked she could repeat in such detail how it happened," recalled Robert Kennedy's wife, Ethel. Jackie's personal physician, Dr. John Walsh, thought it would be good for her to talk about the day. "It's the best way," he said. "Let her get rid of it if she can." A few hours later, fearing that she would collapse from exhaustion, Dr. Walsh injected her with a powerful sedative. It had no impact. He said it was as if he had injected her with Coca-Cola.[6]

In an instant her world had changed. She worried what it would be like to raise her children without a father. "Bobby is going to teach John," she said. "He's a little boy without a father, he's a boyish boy, he'll need a man." She knew that she would have to vacate the White House now that her husband was dead. Her plan was to move back into the Georgetown house they occupied while Jack was in the Senate. "That was the first thing I thought that night — where will I go? I wanted my old house back." Defense secretary Robert McNamara, a former president of Ford Motor Company, offered to buy back the house for her, but already she was having second thoughts. "I thought — how can I go back there to that bedroom[?]"[7]

While she was waiting for the autopsy and embalming at Bethesda Naval Hospital, Mrs. Kennedy called a family friend, artist William Walton, and asked him to consult a book of sketchings showing Lincoln's lying-in-state at the White House. She wanted her husband's viewing and funeral modeled after Lincoln's. Historian and Kennedy aide Arthur Schlesinger Jr. and speechwriter Richard Goodwin rushed to the Library of Congress and spent the night researching other details of the Lincoln rites.

CHAPTER 12:

"You Have Been Charged"

At 11:50 p.m., Police Chief Jesse Curry, District Attorney Henry Wade, and Captain J.W. Fritz stepped into the third-floor hallway to tell reporters that they had filed charges against Oswald in the assassination of the president. Assaulted by questions from skeptical reporters who wanted to see Oswald, they discussed making arrangements for the press to see the prisoner. A nearby microphone picked up fragments of the conversation. "We could take him to the show up room," Fritz said, referring to the room where Oswald had just stood in three lineups, "and put him on the stage and let him stand there. They couldn't, of course, interview him from up there, you know, but if you want them to look at him or take his picture — I'm not sure whether we should or shouldn't." Curry supported the move. "We've got the assembly room," he is recorded as saying. "We could go down there."

Curry told the Warren Commission that he invited the media to see Oswald on the evening of November 22 in the hopes that they might recognize him. Rattled by the possibility that they had uncovered an international communist conspiracy to decapitate the United States government, Curry worried that Oswald still had accomplices on the loose. Perhaps he had been stalking Kennedy and one of the reporters covering the president would not only have seen Oswald, they may have seen him with other people. The main reason, however, was to prove to the world that Oswald was not being mistreated.[1]

At 12:10 a.m., detectives led Oswald out of the interrogation room and down to the basement where the world press would get their first sustained look at the man now officially charged with assassinating the president of the United States. Oswald was led out into the narrow, crowded corridor. Standing in the hallway, just a few feet away, was his future assassin. Ruby despised Oswald for shooting his president. But the thought of killing the suspected assassin had not yet entered his mind. Oddly enough, seeing Oswald in person for the first time in person, Ruby thought he was good-looking and resembled actor Paul Newman.[2]

Conspiracy advocates have tried, unconvincingly, to make the case that Ruby was a mob hit man sent to silence Oswald. These theories are based on unproved allegations and wild speculation. Most of all, they fail to explain why Ruby did not shoot Oswald on Friday night in the midst of the confusion at the police station. Ruby stood a few feet away from Oswald, and he appeared to have a gun in his pocket, but he made no effort to kill him. He had no way of knowing whether he would get another shot at him. Why would he pass up the opportunity?

Police pushed Oswald past Ruby, maneuvering him onto the elevator that brought him to the downstairs assembly room. With members of the press fighting for position and flash bulbs popping, police escorted Oswald onto the stage. The understanding was the reporters would get to see the prisoner to confirm that police were not abusing him, but there would be no questions.

Reporters, and virtually everyone else who happened to be in police headquarters at the time, stood only inches from Oswald. None had been searched for weapons or had credentials checked. Ruby followed Oswald down to the crowded basement and climbed on top of a table in the back of the room, clearly visible on film. Local law enforcement officers all knew Ruby, and they were aware that he was not a reporter, but none found it unusual that he was in the room. Dallas FBI agent Vincent Drain recalled seeing Jack Ruby. He even spoke with him. I "really didn't think anything about it," he recalled later.[3]

When asked if he killed the president, Oswald responded, "No, I have not been charged with that. In fact nobody has said that to me yet. The first thing I heard about it was when the newspaper reporter in the hall

. . . asked me the question." "You have been charged," a reporter in the front told him. "Sir?" Oswald responded, looking confused. "You have been charged," the reporter repeated. Before Oswald could respond, Curry decided to shut down the impromptu meeting. Two detectives pushed Oswald toward the exit as frantic reporters tried to get in a few more questions.

Observing Oswald that evening, motorcycle officer Bobby Joe Dale felt that it was the suspect and not the officials who demonstrated poise and confidence. "When Oswald would come out of the office and down the hall, what I observed was that he seemed to be toying with everybody," he reflected. "He was way ahead of everybody else. He knew what he was doing and seemed very confident. He acted like he was in charge and, as it turned out, he probably was."[4]

· · ·

When the press conference ended Ruby walked outside and saw District Attorney Henry Wade. "Hi, Henry," he shouted. When Wade asked him what he was doing there, Ruby replied, "I know all these fellows," referring to reporters. He then introduced himself to Justice of the Peace David Johnston, who had just filed charges on Oswald, and gave him a pass to his club, the Carousel.

Ruby looked on as Wade tried to respond to the rapid-fire questions of a group of reporters who had surrounded him outside the basement assembly room.

"Does he have a lawyer?" "Does he appear sane to you?"

While Wade struggled to answer, a reporter asked if Oswald was a member of any communist organization.

"Well," Wade replied, "the only one I mentioned was the Free Cuba movement or whatever that . . . "

Before he could finish his answer, Ruby jumped into the conversation, shouting, "Fair Play for Cuba Committee." Wade accepted the correction.

Conspiracy theorists have seen this exchange as proof that Ruby had detailed knowledge of Oswald's background, suggesting that he was more than a just casual observer. In fact, media outlets — both television and radio — had made numerous references to Oswald's association with the group. Ruby was likely parroting what he had heard on the radio earlier in the evening.[5]

• • •

After the press conference, police escorted Oswald to the fourth-floor jail, where he was searched again and booked, nearly eleven hours after his arrest. As he stepped off the elevator, a clerk and another police officer greeted Oswald. They removed his handcuffs and instructed him to empty his pockets, which had already been searched. As he was being checked into the jail Oswald struck up a casual conversation with one of the detectives. Seemingly oblivious to the circumstances surrounding his incarceration, Oswald spoke about his wife and his children before asking the officer if he had any kids. He told him about his life in Russia. It was hard, he confessed, but it was better than most Americans believed. The detective, seeing an opening, asked Oswald if he owned a rifle in Russia. Oswald refused to take the bait.[6]

The clerk behind the counter asked one of the detectives to go back downstairs and retrieve any items that had already been taken from Oswald. All these items were then placed in an envelope, which would be returned to the prisoner in the unlikely event he was released. The clerk was instructed to place Oswald in maximum-security cell F-2 with two guards on duty at all times.[7]

In keeping with policy, Oswald was instructed to turn over his clothes. "What clothes?" Oswald asked. "Everything comes off but the shorts and socks." Oswald seemed shocked by the request. "I don't have to undress," he insisted, but soon relented and started unbuttoning his shirt. "They told me I can use a phone," Oswald said. The clerk told him there were phones down the hall and he would have a chance to make a call in due time. As the conversation continued Oswald removed his shoes and his pants. The clerk shoved the clothes into a large paper bag. "When they want you downstairs again," he said, "you just come here and pick up your clothes." Oswald stood before him wearing only shorts and socks.[8]

The guard took Oswald by the arm and led him onto the elevator and up to the fifth floor, which housed the maximum-security cells. "I want a lawyer," Oswald protested. "I know my rights." The guard, used to hearing similar pleas, simply ignored him. They walked through another locked door and into a narrow hall with a wall on the right side and three prison cells on the left. Oswald was placed in the center cell. There were four bunk beds, two on each side. Along the back wall of the cell doors stood a porcelain sink and a toilet.[9]

From the time Oswald entered custody until he was put into his jail cell at 12:20 a.m. on November 23, he had nothing to eat. He was offered food and water but refused. At one point during the evening he drank a cup of coffee. He never asked to shower.[10]

At 12:35 a.m., Oswald had been in a cell less than ten minutes when police summoned him across the hall to be photographed and finger-printed. "I have been fingerprinted," Oswald protested. Oswald was refer-ring to the prints he gave around 9:00 p.m. for comparison with the prints discovered on the rifle and cardboard boxes found on the sixth floor. Now that felony charges had been filed against him, the police needed more permanent prints. Oswald proved petulant and irritable. He dragged his fingers across the ink pad, forcing the clerk to take each digit one by one and roll them across the pad. When they asked him to sign his name at the

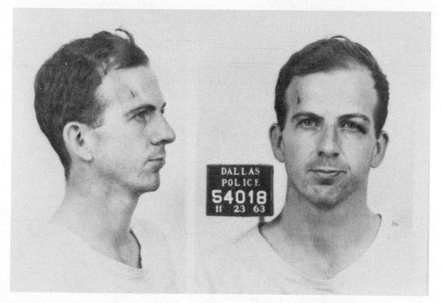

bottom of the fingerprint card, Oswald refused. He then posed for his now famous mug shot — front and profile. The whole procedure took about thirty-five minutes before police took Oswald back to his fifth-floor cell.

He had little time to rest. Shortly before 1:30 a.m., the clerk handed Oswald his clothes and told him to get dressed. Two officers escorted him back to the fourth floor, this time to be arraigned for the murder of President Kennedy. "Well, I guess this is the trial," he said as he entered the room packed with law enforcement officers. Justice of the Peace Johnston advised Oswald of his constitutional right to remain silent and warned him that any statement he made could be used as evidence against him. He then read the complaint charging Oswald with the assassination of President Kennedy. "Lee Harvey Oswald, hereafter styled Defendant, heretofore on or about the twenty-second day of November, 1963, in the County of Dallas and State of Texas, did then and there unlawfully, voluntarily, and with malice aforethought kill John F. Kennedy by shooting him with a gun against the peace and dignity of the State." Oswald remained defiant. "I don't know what you're talking about," he said. "That is the deal, is it?" he repeated that he wanted Mr. John Abt of New York to represent him and he proceeded to spell out his name "A-B-T."[11]

The proceeding took about ten minutes before Oswald was returned to his cell for the night.

· · ·

While Oswald was sleeping investigators were uncovering important evidence in the case. Most significantly, they were able to find the original order for the rifle that was used in the assassination. They discovered that it came from Klein's Sporting Goods in Chicago and was shipped by parcel post in March 1963. The envelope was addressed to "A. Hidell." The police could now trace the murder weapon to Oswald, or at least to one of his aliases. The next day, when police released the information, NBC News anchor David Brinkley snarled: "The president was killed by some punk with a mail order rifle."[12]

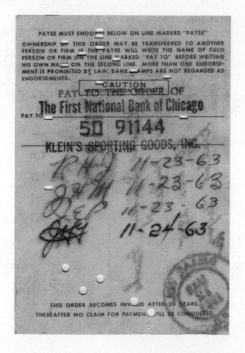

A few officers in the Dallas police station, frustrated that Oswald was so defiant, had discussed their own scheme for getting a confession. An assistant sheriff concocted a plan to invade Oswald's cell while he slept and threaten him with more traditional Dallas justice. "You're going to the electric chair," they planned to tell him. "[W]ould you rather burn as a cop killer or for an ideal?" In addition to scaring the hell out of the suspect, the threat was designed to play to Oswald's ego. Perhaps the threat of death, coupled with the opportunity to talk about his "ideals," would entice a confession. It's unclear why the assault never took place, but the presence of the world's media likely played a role.[13]

...

Oswald managed to sleep; Jack Ruby did not. After hanging out at the police headquarters for a few more hours, Ruby drove to a local radio station, where he finally delivered his sandwiches and sodas. He arrived at 1:50 a m.

Ike Pappas, who had met Ruby earlier in the evening when he helped introduce him to Wade, was at the station working on a story when the nightclub owner strutted in with two bags of food. "Hi guys," he said, "I thought you guys would be working late and you might [want] some coffee or Cokes. I've got some sandwiches here." Pappas thought to himself: "There's that weird guy again. He's everywhere." Pappas did not trust Ruby so he refused to eat the sandwiches — "I didn't know what he had put in them," he reflected — but he did drink a Coke.[14]

Ruby left the radio station at 2:30 a.m., and after spending an hour sitting in a parking lot talking with a police officer and a stripper from his club, he continued on to the *Dallas Times Herald* building. He arrived at 4 a.m. to check on his ads for the following day. Talking with several of the employees, he complained that Oswald was "a little weasel of a guy."[15]

At 4:30 a.m. he left the *Times Herald* building and returned home. But he was too agitated to sleep. Instead, he woke up his roommate, George Senator. "The next thing I knew," recalled Senator, "somebody was hollering at me, shaking me up, [and it was] Ruby. He was excited. He was moody; and the first thing come [*sic*] out of his mouth is . . . 'Gee, his four children and Mrs. Kennedy, what a terrible thing to happen.'" Ruby also complained about an "Impeach Earl Warren" poster. With Senator in tow, Ruby went to take pictures of the poster, which he believed had to be the work of "commies or birchers." Hoping to find an address for the mysterious person responsible for the poster, he headed to the post office, but was told to come back during regular hours. After a stop for breakfast at the Southland Hotel Coffee Shop, Ruby returned home and finally went to sleep at 6:00 a.m., just a few hours before Oswald woke up.[16]

· · ·

At 3:30 a.m., doctors at Bethesda Naval Hospital finished their painstaking work on the president's head wound. Kennedy's valet, George Thomas, brought clothes. "He had four summer suits and four winter suits, and two good pairs of brown shoes and two good black pairs." They agreed on a blue-gray suit and a blue tie. They placed a white handkerchief in his pocket. At 3:56 a.m., the coffin was loaded into a hearse for the thirty-five minute drive back to the White House.[17]

The family arrived back at the White House with the body of President Kennedy at 4:35 that morning. Workers spent most of the night and the early morning preparing the East Room for the viewing. Arthur Schlesinger described the scene as Kennedy returned to the White House for the last time. "The casket was carried into the East Room and deposited on a stand. It was wrapped in a flag. Jackie followed, accompanied by Bobby. . . . A priest said a few words. Then Bobby whispered to Jackie. Then she walked away. The rest of us followed."

Jackie went to her room, but Bobby returned and asked Schlesinger to view the body and make a recommendation about whether to have an open casket. He recorded his thoughts in his journal later that day. "And so I went in, with the candles fitfully burning, three priests on their knees praying in the background, and took a last look at my beloved President, my beloved friend," he wrote. "For a moment, I was shattered. But it was not a good job, probably it could not have been with half his head blasted away. It was too waxen, too made up. It did not really look like him." Schlesinger reported back to Bobby who made the decision to have a closed coffin.[18]

CHAPTER 13:

"My Wife and I Like the President's Family"

Guards woke Lee Harvey Oswald at 8:00 a.m. Saturday morning for breakfast. It was a short sleep, since it was nearly 2:00 a.m. when they finally locked him in his solitary cell. The breakfast was standard city jail cuisine: stewed apricots, oatmeal, plain bread, and black coffee. There was no mention of Oswald taking a shower. The guards did not trust Oswald with a razor, probably because they feared he would use it to commit suicide, so one of the jailers shaved him.[1]

...

While Oswald sat in his jail cell waiting for his morning interrogation session, the city of Washington was grappling with the consequences of his actions. At 10:00 a.m., about seventy-five Kennedy family members and close friends attended what many believed was the first Catholic mass ever held in the White House. "The whole family was like a bunch of shipwreck survivors," said JFK friend Lem Billings. "I don't think they could have made it at all without Bobby. He seemed to be everywhere. He always had an arm around a friend or family member and was telling them it was okay, that it was time to move ahead."[2]

At 10:01 a.m., as the Kennedy family gathered for mass, President Johnson received a briefing from FBI head J. Edgar Hoover. "I just wanted to let you know of a development which I think is very important in connection with this case," Hoover announced in his staccato voice. "The evidence that they have at the present time is not very, very strong." The FBI lab was testing the gun and the bullets, and they were able to prove that Oswald, using the alias "A. Hidell" had purchased the gun from a sporting goods store in Chicago. "But the important thing is that this gun was bought in Chicago on a money order — cost $21 — and it seems almost impossible to think that for $21 you could kill the president of the United States." The actual price was $21.45. Oswald paid $12.78 for the rifle, $7.17 for the telescopic sight, and $1.50 for postage and handling.[3]

Johnson was clearly worried about the possible Soviet connection, and he pumped Hoover for information. "Have you established any more about the visit to the Soviet embassy in Mexico in September?" he asked. Hoover had no new information to offer, but he revealed that the FBI routinely read all of the mail sent to the Soviet Embassy in Washington. They had intercepted a letter from Oswald complaining that the FBI was harassing his wife. There was nothing incriminating in the letter, however. "The case as it stands now isn't strong enough to be able to get a conviction," Hoover informed Johnson.[4]

At this point, Johnson assumed that Oswald used the same gun to kill Officer Tippit. "That is an entirely different gun," Hoover told him. "You think he might have two?" Johnson asked. Hoover said that Oswald used a revolver to shoot the officer. Johnson concluded with a request that Hoover provide him with a written synopsis and keep him informed of any new developments.

• • •

As Johnson finished his phone call, police in Dallas were preparing the third floor for Oswald's entrance. At 10:25 a.m., a deputy informed reporters that they were to ask no questions of Oswald. A few minutes later, the suspect appeared, surrounded by officers. The reporters obeyed their orders and refrained from shouting questions.[5]

Oswald entered an interrogation room packed with new faces: FBI and Secret Service agents from both Dallas and Washington, along with a Dallas U.S. Marshal, and Dallas detectives. FBI agent Bookhout noted that

Oswald appeared less belligerent then he had the previous day, but he still refused to discuss anything related to the investigation.[6]

As usual, Captain Fritz took the lead in asking questions. As Oswald sat down in the chair for what promised to be another long day of questioning, Fritz asked him how he had slept. "Never slept better," Oswald responded.[7]

Fritz now had enough evidence to start exposing the contradictions in Oswald's story. He began by asking whether he took curtain rods to work. Oswald denied it. "Well, the fella that drove you to work yesterday morning tells us that you had a package in the back seat," Fritz said. "I didn't have any kind of package," Oswald responded. "I don't know what he's talking about. I had my lunch and that's all I had."[8]

Believing Frazier's account, Fritz kept probing Oswald on the specifics. He asked Oswald if he had mentioned anything to Frazier about curtain rods. "No," Oswald responded. He also emphatically denied ever saying that he picked up rods from Mrs. Paine's house or carried a package into the depository building that morning.

Fritz managed to expose some minor discrepancies in Oswald's story, but they did not amount to much. Oswald previously claimed that he took a bus back to his rooming house, but Fritz knew that Oswald in fact took a taxi. When he pointed out the contradiction, Oswald backtracked. "Actually, I did board a bus at the book depository but after a block or two it got stalled in traffic, so I got off and took a cab back to my room." Once again, Oswald demonstrated an instinctive ability to know when to concede a point when Fritz had evidence to expose his lies, and when he was fishing for information. Only electing to answer questions that did not incriminate him, Oswald was, to be sure, a tough nut to crack.[9]

Still, Captain Fritz remained tenacious in his pursuit of Oswald's confession. He probed Oswald about his actions around the time of the assassination. "Did you eat lunch with anyone yesterday?" Oswald claimed he ate with two "colored" employees. One was named Junior; he could not recall the other name. This was the first Fritz had heard mention of two potential witnesses who could prove Oswald's innocence. But curiously, he did not pursue the lead. (Both men would later deny having lunch with Oswald.) When asked what he ate for lunch, Oswald responded he had a cheese sandwich and an apple.[10]

Changing course, Fritz enquired about where Oswald stored his belongings. Oswald explained that he kept most of his stuff in the garage at the Paine house. It consisted of two sea bags, a couple of suitcases, a few boxes of kitchen utensils, and some clothes.[11]

"What about a rifle?" Fritz asked. Oswald seemed annoyed by the question. "I didn't store a rifle there," he snapped. [12]

Fritz knew Oswald was lying, but it was also clear that he intended to stick to his story. Trying a different approach, Fritz gave Oswald a break by asking him an innocent question — the kind that Oswald actually liked to answer. "Lee, do you have any other friends or relatives living nearby?" Oswald mentioned his brother, Robert, and the Paines. Fritz then maneuvered back to the main thread of questioning. Did he order guns through the mail? Did he own a gun? Oswald denied that he ever ordered a gun or owned one.[12]

The police already determined that the rifle had been purchased from Klein's Sporting Goods in Chicago and had been shipped to a person using the name of A. Hidell. At this point, FBI agent Bookhout joined in the questioning. Why would he have a card with a different name on it? Oswald admitted that he carried the card, but he refused responsibility for scrawling the signature on the back. He also stubbornly refused to explain why he carried the card in the first place, or how he may have used it. Secret Service agent Sorrels described Oswald's attitude as "arrogant" and "defiant."[14]

Fritz asked Oswald about his politics. "I don't have any," he responded, before contradicting himself. "I am a member of the Fair Play for Cuba Committee. They have offices in New York, but I was a secretary of the New Orleans chapter when I lived there." Without provocation, Oswald volunteered, "I support the Castro revolution."

"Do you belong to the Communist Party?"

"No, I never had a card. I belong to the American Civil Liberties Union and I paid five dollars dues."

"Why did you carry that pistol into the show?"

"I told you why. I don't want to talk about it anymore. I bought it several months ago in Fort Worth and that's all."

Once again, as soon as Fritz asked questions directly relevant to the case, Oswald stopped cooperating. "I'm not going to answer any more questions about the pistol or any guns until I've talked to a lawyer," he insisted.[15]

Impressed by the way Oswald navigated his questions, Fritz asked Oswald if he had ever been questioned before. "Oh yes. I've been questioned by the FBI for a long time. They use different methods. There is the hard way, the soft way, the buddy method — I'm familiar with all of them. Right now, I don't have to answer any questions until I speak to my attorney."[16]

Fritz reassured him that he could have an attorney anytime he wanted. "I don't have the money to call Mr. Abt," he said. "Call him collect or you could have another lawyer if you want. You can arrange it upstairs," Fritz responded. The detective clearly did not want Oswald to have a lawyer present during the interrogation, and he was probably relieved that the suspect insisted that a lawyer from New York represent him. He could pretend to be satisfying Oswald's request, while continuing to question him without a lawyer.

Fritz quickly changed the subject, perhaps fearful that Oswald would demand to see a local lawyer. "Ever been arrested before?" Fritz asked. "I was in a little trouble with the Fair Play for Cuba thing in New Orleans," Oswald responded. "I had a street fight with some anti-Castro Cubans. We had a debate on a New Orleans radio station."

Getting nowhere with that line of questioning, Fritz tried probing for a possible motive. "What do you think of President Kennedy and his family?" he asked. "I have no views on the president. My wife and I like the president's family. They're interesting people. Of course, I have my own views on the president's national policy. And I have a right to express my views but because of the charges, I don't think I should comment further." Fritz wanted to know if anything about the president bothered Oswald. "I am not a malcontent," he insisted.[17]

Oswald bristled when Fritz suggested that he take a lie detector test. "Not without the advice of counsel. I refused to take one for the FBI in 1962, and I certainly don't intend to take one for the Dallas police."[18]

Fritz then turned the floor over to the other people in the room. The Secret Service interrogator lacked Fritz's' soft approach. Assuming a more aggressive approach, he asked Oswald if he shot the president. "No, I did not," Oswald responded. "Did you shoot the governor?' Oswald says, "No,

I didn't know that the governor had been shot." With that Fritz called the session to an end and sent Oswald back to his cell.[19]

As he was again paraded past the reporters, Oswald pleaded for legal help. "I would like to contact Mr. Abt," he begged, before proceeding to spell it for reporters: "A-B-T."[20]

•••

Oswald's pleas were being heard in Washington. The possibility that the Dallas police were denying Oswald legal representation frightened Assistant Attorney General Nicholas Katzenbach. "My nightmare was that the president's assassin would be convicted and then the Supreme Court would throw the case out because he had not had a lawyer," he told author William Manchester. "I felt that was about as low as we could sink." Katzenbach then contacted the Dallas Bar Association to make certain that Oswald had representation.[21]

•••

While Oswald sat in his cell, Lyndon Johnson received the latest intelligence report about Oswald and his possible ties to foreign groups from CIA director John McCone. LBJ was told that Mexican officials were holding Silvia Duran, a Cuban embassy official who had spoken with Oswald when he visited there on September 27. Duran was being interrogated about possible connections to Oswald.[22]

It is unclear how much detail McCone shared with Johnson, but by Saturday morning many in the CIA were suspecting a possible Soviet plot to kill Kennedy. The CIA station in Mexico City had observed Oswald visiting the Soviet embassy six weeks before the assassination. While visiting the embassy, Oswald had met with Valery Vladimirovich Kostikov, a senior KGB official who specialized in sabotage and assassination. "Putting it baldly," a senior CIA official wrote in a memo, "was Oswald, wittingly or unwittingly, part of a plot to murder President Kennedy in Dallas as an attempt to further exacerbate sectional strife and render the U.S. government less capable of dealing with Soviet initiatives over the next year?"

This news represented another troubling wrinkle in the Oswald story. If the information was correct, and if it became public, how would the nation react? Would Americans demand retaliation? "We could have had a very nasty situation," recalled CIA covert operations chief Richard Helms. "What would be the retaliation? A startled America could do some extreme things. . . . We needed to be careful." For now, Johnson asked to be kept informed of any developments.[23]

CHAPTER 14:

"Brother, You Won't Find Anything There"

Shortly before 1:15 p.m., police handed Oswald his clothes and told him to get dressed. He had visitors. He was escorted down to the fourth floor and into a rectangular room. Heavy glass separated the room into two halves — one for prisoners and one for visitors. There were eight or nine cubicles, each equipped with a phone. As he walked toward one of the booths Oswald could see his wife and mother on the other side.

As evidence mounted against her husband on Friday, Marina confronted the realistic possibility that he really had shot the president. His behavior had been odd, and how else could she explain the missing rifle in the garage? Marina made two additional incriminating discoveries on Friday evening. In sweeping the house of her belongings, the police had left two items behind. One was a small Russian cup that her grandmother had given her. When she looked inside she found Lee's wedding ring. Lee had never before removed his ring. Why on this day?[1]

In addition to the wedding ring, she discovered two small photographs of Lee that she had placed in June's baby book, which the police had also left behind. The black-and-white photos showed Lee in the backyard of a house they had rented on Neely Street. He is pictured holding the Carcano rifle — the same one he was accused of using to assassinate President Kennedy — with his pistol tucked in his pants. (She did not know that the police had found copies of the photos from the boxes they had removed from the garage.)

Despite the discoveries, Marina had convinced herself that Lee was innocent. But what should she do with this new evidence? She could not share it with the police, so she decided to tuck the two photographs into the shoes she was wearing. Perhaps she believed that she would be able to give them to Lee, or have a secret conversation where he could tell her what to do with them.

Marina eagerly picked up the phone. Lee seemed happy to see his wife, but not his mother. "Why did you bring that fool with you?" he asked. "I don't want to talk to her." Marina, trying to play peacemaker, responded, "She's your mother. Of course she came." She noticed his swollen eye and other cuts and wondered if the police had been abusing him. "Oh, no, they treat me fine. You're not to worry about that. Did you bring Junie and Rachel?"[2]

Marina told him that the children were with her at the police station. She, however, was eager to talk to him about everything that had just taken place. "Alka," she said, using his Russian nickname, "can we talk about anything we like?" He responded sarcastically, "Oh, of course. We can speak about *absolutely* anything at all." She could tell by his tone that he was saying exactly the opposite: that she should be careful about what she said. She knew now not to tell him about the photos. "They asked me about the gun," she told him. "Oh, that's nothing," he replied dismissively, "and you're not to worry if there's a trial. It's a mistake. I'm not guilty. There are people who will help me." He told her about the lawyer in New York whom he was trying to reach.[3]

Marina started to cry. "Don't cry," he said. "Ah, don't cry. There's nothing to cry about. Try not to think about it. Everything is going to be all right. And if they ask you anything, you have a right not to answer. You have the right to refuse. Do you understand?" She could not bring herself to ask him if he did it. She noticed that he had tears in his eyes as he spoke with her. Their entire conversation was in Russian.[4]

Marina then handed the phone to Oswald's mother. She recalled that her son "seemed very calm, very normal, and sure of himself." She asked about the bruises on his face. "Honey, you are so bruised up, your face. What are they doing?" He assured her it was nothing. "Mother, don't worry. I got that in a scuffle." She was convinced that he was being beaten up while in jail. "Is there anything I can do to help you?" "No, mother, everything is fine. I know my rights and I will have an attorney. . . . Don't worry about a thing."[5]

With the time running down Marina got back on the phone. Lee again reassured her that everything would be okay. "You have friends. They'll help you. If it comes to that, you can ask the Red Cross for help. You mustn't worry about me. Kiss June and Rachel for me." As the guards entered the room to take him away she spoke her last words to him. "Remember that I love you." Lee told Marina that he loved her very much and to make sure to buy shoes for June. He walked backwards out of the room so that he could see her until the last second.[6]

Assuming that Lee was innocent, Marina had entered the room looking for signs to support her faith. She found none. After seeing him, listening to the tone of his voice, and studying the expression on his face, she became convinced that he was guilty. She saw it in his eyes. Had he been innocent, the Lee that she knew would have been screaming about his rights and condemning the police for illegally detaining him. The fact that he told her that everything was going to be "all right" was the clearest sign that he was in fact guilty.[7]

After the meeting with his wife and mother, Oswald was briefly returned to his cell. After spending a few minutes lying in the top bunk Oswald heard the security door open and the jail guard Jim Popplewell approaching the cell. They had received permission from Captain Fritz to allow Oswald to make a phone call. The guards opened the cell door and Oswald, wearing only shorts and socks, was escorted down the hall where there were two telephones in glass booths. Popplewell handed Oswald a dime, placed him inside the booth, and then locked the door behind him. Oswald wanted to call an attorney in New York but he did not know how to make a long-distance phone call.

An operator told Oswald to deposit his dime and dial 212-555-1212. Oswald followed the instructions, informing the operator that he was trying to reach John Abt. He spelled the name for the operator. She gave Oswald the number, which he repeated out loud, and then hung up the phone. But he quickly forgot the number and asked Popplewell for a piece of paper and a pencil. The officer tore the corner from a telephone contact slip and handed it to Oswald along with a pencil. Oswald needed to make the phone call again but he had used his only dime. He protested that he had $13 taken from him and that he should be able to use it to make a phone call. He was told it was policy to give a prisoner a dime to make one call.[8]

Oswald reached the long-distance operator again and asked if he could make a collect call. The call, however, was refused. Oswald wanted to call home to ask his wife to contact Abt, but he was not allowed to make another call. With that, Popplewell unlocked the booth and led Oswald back to his cell.

What he did not know was that Abt and his wife had gone to their Connecticut cabin for the weekend. He would not learn of Oswald's request until the next day. By then, Lee Harvey Oswald was dead.

• • •

At 2:15 p.m. on Saturday, November 23, Oswald was brought down for another lineup. On the other side of the screen stood W. W. Scoggins, the cab driver who witnessed the shooting of officer Tippit. Also on the lineup was William Wayne Whaley, the cab driver who drove Oswald from the Greyhound bus station to his boarding home.[9]

This time Oswald was handcuffed to three other prisoners and he was number three in the lineup. The night before the police had removed Oswald's shirt for testing. He was upset, claiming that the police were preventing him from putting on a shirt over his T-shirt. "I've been photographed in a T-shirt and now they're taking me to a lineup among these men. Naturally, I will be picked out. Right?" Even as they're brought out into the bright lights Oswald was still complaining. "It's not right to put me in line with these teenagers. I know what you're doing. You're trying to railroad me! I want my lawyer!"[10]

The witnesses harbored little doubt that Oswald was the man they saw. The taxi driver immediately identified Oswald. "That's him all right." Scoggins was even more emphatic: "Well, he can bitch and holler all he wants, but that's the man I saw running from the scene. Number three."[11]

After the lineup, police returned Oswald to his cell. A detective obtained scrapings from under his fingernails along with specimens of hair from his head, armpit, chest, forearm, pubic area, and right leg. The specimens were sent for analysis to the FBI lab in Washington, D.C.[12]

• • •

While Oswald stood in the lineup, Captain Fritz mentioned to Chief Curry that "this case is cinched. This man killed the president, there is no question in my mind about it." A few minutes later, Fritz repeated the same line to NBC reporter Tom Pettit who went live from Dallas. He quoted Fritz as saying: "This man killed the president — we have a cinched case against him."[13]

At that point Chief Curry was eager to move Oswald to the county jail, and to do so as early as 4:00 p.m. — two hours away. "Can he be ready by about four o'clock? Can he be transferred by four o'clock?" Curry asked. Fritz was not ready to give up on the possibility of getting a confession, telling Curry he could not have Oswald ready by 4:00 p.m. Would he be ready by 10:00 a.m. on Sunday morning, Curry asked, "so I could tell these people something definitely?" Fritz was confident that he would be finished with Oswald by then. Curry then told a group of reporters that "if you men will be here by no later than ten o'clock in the morning, why . . . that will be early enough."[14]

Word had already circulated that Oswald was going to be transferred and some reporters moved down to the basement in the hopes of catching a glimpse of Oswald on his way to the county jail.

• • •

One of the people planning to be there was Jack Ruby. After waking up at 10:30 a.m., Ruby ate breakfast and watched television coverage of the assassination until 1:00 p.m., when he went to the Carousel Club. Listening to the news reports, he heard the rumors that Chief Curry planned to transfer Oswald at 4:00 p.m. He called a local radio station and talked to the announcer about the transfer. "You know I'll be there," he said.

Ruby left his club at 3:00 p.m. and drove to Dealey Plaza, where he watched as people laid wreaths at the site of the Kennedy shooting. From there he ventured over to the third floor of police headquarters. He would later deny being there, likely to avoid the charge of premeditated murder. The Warren Commission could not decide whether Ruby had been there or not, but a number of eyewitnesses claimed to have seen him. As usual, Ruby gave out business cards to reporters. Sticking around police headquarters until nearly 6:00 p.m., Ruby only left after Curry announced to reporters that the transfer had been delayed until Sunday morning.[15]

• • •

At 3:37 p.m., police escorted Oswald down to the fourth floor to see his brother, Robert. The two men had not seen each other for almost a year. They had not spoken in the previous eight months. When he learned that his brother had been arrested and was considered a suspect in the assassination of the president, Robert left his job at the Acme Brick company and drove to the police station in Dallas in hopes of seeing his brother or talking to Captain Fritz about the charges. "If Lee were innocent, of course, I would do everything I could to free him," he recalled. "If he were guilty, I would try to discover why he had fired the shots."[16]

Robert failed to achieve either goal on Friday, but he returned on Saturday after police promised him a chance to see his brother. After a long delay, a Secret Service agent led Robert to an elevator that took him to the fourth floor. He walked through a door, and down a long narrow room, where he sat in front of a heavy glass partition waiting for his brother.

Robert recalled watching Lee casually strolling toward the partition. Lee motioned for him to pick up the telephone. In a very calm voice he explained to his brother, "this is taped." Shocked by Lee's appearance, Robert asked if the police had been roughing him up. "I got this at the theater. They haven't bothered me since. They're treating me all right," he assured his brother. As Lee talked, Robert was struck by how completely relaxed he seemed. "He seemed at first to me to be very mechanical," Robert told William Manchester in 1964. Lee was oblivious to the consequences of his actions. "His voice was calm and he talked matter-of-factly, without any sign of tension or strain, as though we were discussing a moderately interesting minor incident at his office or my office."[17]

Lee did not want to talk about the reason why he was in jail.

"What did you think of the baby?" he said, referring to his infant, Rachel.

"Yeah," Robert responded with a sarcastic tone, "Thanks a lot for telling me about the baby. I didn't even know you had one."

Lee smiled: "Well, it was a girl, and I wanted a boy, but you know how that goes."

After more banter about the baby and Marina, Robert was eager to get to the point. "Lee, what the Sam Hill is going on?"

"I don't know."

"You don't know? Look, they've got your pistol, they got your rifle, they've got you charged with shooting the president and a police officer. And you tell me you don't know. Now, I want to know just what's going on."

"I just don't know what you're talking about. Don't believe all this so-called evidence."

Robert studied his brother's face, staring intently into his eyes searching for an explanation in his expression. Lee realized what he was doing and said quietly, "Brother, you won't find anything there."

Lee once again switched the subject, returning to Marina. It seemed odd to Robert that Lee was so concerned about Marina and the kids. If he cared so much about them why did he put them in this predicament? "What do you think she's going to do now, with those kids," asked Robert. "My friends will take care of them," Lee replied. "Do you mean the Paines?" Robert asked. "Yes," Lee responded. Robert, who had already developed an instinctive dislike of both Michael and Ruth, responded: "I don't think they're any friends of yours."

Changing the subject again, Lee turned the discussion to his daughter. "Junie needs a new pair of shoes." Robert had noticed on Friday night that one of the red tennis shoes she was wearing had worn through at the toe. Lee had made the same comment when talking to his mother and Marina. "Don't worry about that," Robert said. "I'll take care of that."

A Secret Service agent had mentioned to Robert that his brother was trying to reach an attorney in New York. "What about this attorney you tried to contact in New York. Who is he?"

"Well, he's just an attorney I want to handle my case."

"I'll get you an attorney down here."

"No, you stay out of it."

"Stay out of it? It looks like I've been dragged into it."

"I'm not going to have anybody from down here. I want this one."

"Well, all right."

After a few more words, Robert watched as a police officer came into the room, tapped Lee on the shoulder, and told him that his time was up. Robert was convinced that if he had just another ten or fifteen minutes to spend quietly talking to his brother he would have been able to get some answers. At the very least, Lee would have indicated to him why he thought it was necessary to assassinate the president.

"If I had been allowed to spend half an hour with Lee that Saturday and then continue our talk over the next day or two, I believe I would have been able to arrive at final answers to two questions: Was Lee guilty? If he was guilty, what were his motives?"

With the police officer hovering, Lee and Robert spoke their last words.

"I'll see you in a day or two," Robert said.

"Now, you've got your job and everything. Don't be running back and forth all the time and get yourself in trouble with your boss."

"Don't worry about that. I'll be back."

"All right," Lee said. "I'll see you."

With that, Oswald was escorted back to his jail cell on the fifth floor.[18]

* * *

At 4:00 p.m., after another unsuccessful attempt to reach the attorney in New York City from the phone booth on the fifth floor, Oswald called Ruth Paine. He gave her explicit instructions on how to reach Mr. Abt. "He's an attorney I would like to have represent me," Oswald told her.

"I would be grateful if you would call him for me."

She was surprised by how calm and matter-of-fact he was, how he seemed detached from all the pain he had caused so many people, herself included, but she agreed to make the call. Oswald hung up and called back a few seconds later. Paine was stunned to hear him repeat his request, nearly word for word, for her to contact Mr. Abt.[19]

At 5:45 p.m., Oswald returned to his jail cell where he received another visitor. It was H. Lewis Nichols, president of the Dallas Bar Association, accompanied by Chief Curry. It is likely that the visit was inspired by a phone call from Assistant Attorney General Nicholas Katzenbach, who had watched Oswald plead for legal representation on national television.

They found Oswald lying on his bunk in his pants and T-shirt. Curry instructed the officer to open Oswald's cell. He introduced Nichols and then moved into the outer hallway to give the two men privacy. Nichols, sitting on the bunk across from Oswald, wanted to make sure that the prisoner was aware of his right to have an attorney. He offered the services of the Dallas Bar Association to help find a lawyer.

Oswald refused the request, reiterating that he would only be represented by John Abt, or by a lawyer from the American Civil Liberties Union. He said that he was a member of the ACLU "and if I can't get Mr. Abt, I would like to have somebody from that organization represent me."

Nichols was convinced that Oswald was in control of his facilities and aware of his rights.

Reporters swarmed Nichols as he exited the elevator on the third floor. "He appeared to be perfectly rational and I could observe no abnormalities about him at all in the short time that I visited with him," he said.[20]

• • •

At 6:24 p.m., Oswald was escorted from his jail cell to the homicide and robbery office for another interrogation session. As he passed the gaggle of reporters he complained about being denied "the basic fundamental hygienic rights like a shower."

In the room for this session was Captain Fritz, Secret Service inspector Thomas Kelley, FBI agent James Bookhout, and Detective Guy Rose. Fritz began, as he often did, by asking a couple of questions designed to put the suspect at ease. Finally, Fritz turned to the business at hand, reminding Oswald that he claimed that he never owned a gun. While searching the Paine's garage, police had come across the famous photograph of Oswald

posing with a rifle. Fritz had the photograph enlarged to make sure there was no confusion about what it contained. "How do you explain this?"[21]

Oswald smugly replied that he would not make any comment without the advice of an attorney. Fritz ignored the comment and pushed further. "Well, is that your face in the picture?" Oswald was defiant: "I won't even admit that." Fritz seemed surprised by Oswald's denial, asking him again if that was his face in the picture. "That is not even my face," he responded. "Well, that's just a fake." After initially saying he would not talk, he could barely contain himself. "I have been through that whole deal with all people in the cameras [*sic*]," he protested. "One has taken my picture and that is my face and put a different body on it."[22]

Fritz saw an opening: Oswald had admitted that it was his face. "So that is your face," he asked. Oswald insisted that the photograph was a forgery. "Someone has taken my picture and that is my face and put a different body on it. I know all about photography, I worked with photography for a long time. That is a picture that someone else has made. I never saw that picture in my life."[23]

Fritz then reached into an envelope and pulled out a small snapshot, the original print that was used to make the enlargement. "I've never seen that picture either. That picture has been reduced from the big one." The conversation then devolved into a debate about who knew more about photography. Oswald remained defiant, insisting that he was being framed, and that the pictures were fake. Fritz could only conclude that Oswald was either the victim of an immense and well-coordinated conspiracy, or he was a psychopathic liar.[24]

After forty-five minutes of fruitless questioning, Fritz ordered guards to return Oswald to his cell.

At 7:15 p.m., police led Oswald through the third-floor hallway back to the elevator to take him to his cell as live television cameras swung around and zoomed in on him. Newsmen rushed toward him, arms outstretched, microphones searching for a brief statement. "Did you fire that rifle?" a reporter shouted. "I don't know what dispatches you people have been given," he warned, "but I emphatically deny these charges!" As officers pulled Oswald through the crowd a reporter asked him about Governor Connally, who was seriously wounded but expected to live.

"I have nothing against anybody," he said. "I have not committed any acts of violence."[25]

• • •

After a few minutes in his cell, Oswald asked permission to make another phone call. At 8:00 p.m. he was escorted to the small phone booth where he placed another call to Ruth Paine. When Ruth answered he asked in Russian to speak with Marina. Marina had left the house and was staying at a local hotel. She and Oswald's mother had made arrangements with *Life* magazine to provide housing in exchange for access to them and their story. Paine told Oswald she did not know where Marina was staying. "Tell her she should be at your house," an irritated Oswald replied. Paine promised to reach her and deliver the message.[26]

Ruth quickly called the hotel and got Marguerite on the phone and told her that Lee was upset that Marina was not at the house. Lee's mom had other priorities. "Well," she responded coldly, "he is in prison, he doesn't know the things we are up against, the things we have to face. What he wants doesn't really matter."[27]

After the phone call, Oswald was served dinner: red beans, bread, and a small salad. He would spend his last evening alone, laying on his narrow cot in the maximum-security cell. He likely knew that he would be transferred to the county jail, but when? Would they move him in the middle of the night to avoid the media? Was it possible that Fritz would make another attempt at gaining a confession in the morning?[28]

While her son was eating his dinner, Marguerite claims to have had a strange encounter with an FBI agent. She said that FBI agent came to the hotel where *Life* magazine was holding Marguerite, Marina, and the two children. The agent showed Marguerite a picture — a mug shot of a man. "Mrs. Oswald," he asked, "have you ever seen this man before?" She responded: "No sir — no sir, believe me, I have never seen this man before." The face was not familiar. It was not until the next day, after her son was dead, that she recognized the man in the mug shot. She claimed it was Jack Ruby.[29]

CHAPTER 15:

"I Don't Know What You Are Talking About"

At 9:30 a.m. on Sunday morning detectives James Leavelle and L.C. Graves went to the fourth-floor jail, handcuffed Oswald in front, and took him down the elevator to the third floor. While on the elevator, Oswald asked where he was going, obviously aware that he would be transferred at some point. He must have been surprised to see that the hallway had been cleared of reporters. They had all relocated to the basement in anticipation of the transfer.[1]

Oswald, still wearing the same white short-sleeved T-shirt, a pair of black trousers, black socks, and loafers that he had on when he was arrested, entered the room surrounded by two guards. They sat him at the table directly across from Dallas postal inspector Harry Holmes. On his way to church that morning, Holmes had learned that Oswald was still in police custody. He had a number of questions he wanted to ask the suspect about the post office boxes he had rented, so he drove to the station and asked Fritz if he could participate in the interrogation session. Fritz obliged.

As he sat down Oswald looked at the faces in the room. In addition to Holmes and Fritz, there were two Secret Service agents, Forrest Sorrels and Thomas Kelley, and two Dallas detectives who stood guard over the suspect. "Are there any FBI men in here?" Oswald asked. Fritz responded, "No, no FBI men." "Well, who is that man?" Oswald said, looking at Holmes. Fritz explained that Holmes was a postal inspector and might have a few questions to ask. Oswald mumbled, "Okay."[2]

Holmes described the interrogation as informal. "One man would question Oswald. Another would interrupt with a different trend of thought, or something in connection, and it was sort of an informal questioning or interrogation."[3] Knowing this was his last chance to get a confession before Oswald was transferred to the county jail, Fritz was more direct. "Did you shoot the president?" "No," Oswald said. "Do you have any knowledge of the shooting?" "No," Oswald replied.

"What about the shooting of Officer Tippit?" Oswald: "Look, I don't know why you're asking me these questions. The only reason I'm here is because I popped a policeman in the nose at the theater on Jefferson Avenue. Okay, I admit it. But the reason I hit him was because I was protecting myself. As far as the rest of it, I emphatically deny having anything to do with shooting an officer or killing the president."[4]

Fritz asked Oswald about the Dallas map that had been recovered from his room — the one that had left assistant district attorney Alexander convinced that the suspect was part of an international conspiracy. Fritz asked about the X's and what they represented.

"Oh my God don't tell me there's a mark near where this thing happened?"

"Why were the X's on there?"

"I have no automobile. I have no means of conveyance. I have to walk from where I am going most of the time. I had my applications in with Texas employment commission. They furnished me names and addresses of places that had openings like I might could fill, and neighborhood people had furnished me information on jobs I might could get. I was seeking a job, and I would put these markings on the map so that I could plan my itinerary around with less walking, and each one of those represented a place where I went and interviewed for a job. You can check each one of them out if you want to."[5]

Fritz then mentioned the X at the intersection of Elm and Houston, which was the scene of the assassination. "That is the location of the Texas school depository and I did go there and interview for a job," he responded. "In fact, I got a job there. That is all the map amounts to."[6]

Someone questioned Oswald about his religious and political beliefs. "I am not a communist," he declared. "I am a Marxist." When they asked him the difference, he explained "a communist is a Lenin Marxist, and I am a true Karl Marxist." A Secret Service agent asked "What religion are you?" Oswald responded, "I have no faith." The conversation then turned to the Bible. "I have read the Bible. It is fair reading, but not very interesting," Oswald opined, his words flowing freely. "But, as a matter of fact, I am a student of philosophy and I don't consider the Bible is even a reasonable or intelligent philosophy. I don't think much of it."[7]

After the digression into politics and religion, Fritz brought the conversation back to the assassination.

"Do you own a rifle?"

"Absolutely not. How would I afford a rifle? I make a $1.25 an hour. I can't hardly feed myself.

"Have you shot a rifle since you have been out of the Marines?"

"No. . . . Well, possibly a small bore, maybe a .22, but nothing larger since I have left the Marine Corps."

"What about this picture of you holding this rifle?"

"Well, I don't know what you are talking about."

None of the exhibits were in the room at the time, and Oswald refused to acknowledge the picture even existed.[8]

The postal inspector wanted to know more about "Alek Hidell."

"Did you receive mail through this box 2915 under the name of any other name than Lee Oswald."

"No, absolutely not."

"Had any come under that name, could this fellow have gotten it?"

"Nobody got mail out of that box but me; no sir. Maybe my wife, but I couldn't say for sure whether my wife ever got mail, but it is possible she could have."

"Well, who is A.J. Hidell?"

"I don't know any such person."

"Have you ever used the name of Alek Hidell?"

"No."

"Well, isn't it true that when you were arrested, you had an ID . . . an identification card with Alek Hidell on it and your picture on it?"

"Yeah, I believe that's right."

"Well, how do you explain that?"

"I don't."⁹

Holmes then showed him the rental box application for the post office box in New Orleans. "Here this shows as being able to receive, being entitled to receive mail, is Marina Oswald."

Oswald responded: "That is my wife. So what?"

Holmes pointed out that it also indicated that "A. J. Hidell" was authorized to receive mail at the box.

"Well, I don't know anything about that."

Holmes wanted to know if anyone else was entitled to get mail at that box.

"No."

"Who did you show as your — what did you show as your business?"

"I didn't show anything."

"Well, your box rental application here says 'Fair Play for Cuba Committee' and the American Civil Liberties Union."

"Maybe that is right, I did put them on there."

"Did they, anyone, pay for the box?"

"I paid for it out of my own personal money."

"Did you rent it in the name of these organizations?"

"No, I don't know why I put it on."

Apparently trying to get Oswald to admit that he was the head of the Fair Play for Cuba Committee, Fritz joined in the questioning. Oswald evaded direct answers, but eventually relented: "Actually, it was a loosely organized thing and we had no officers, but probably you could call me the secretary of it because I did collect money." He elaborated, "In New York they have a well organized or a better organization."

"Is that why you came to Dallas, to organize a cell of this organization in Dallas?"

"No, not at all."

"Did you work on it or intend to organize here in Dallas?"

"No, I didn't. I was too busy trying to get a job."¹⁰

Secret Service agent Kelley, wanting to pursue whether Oswald may have been part of a larger conspiracy, asked Oswald about his connections to political groups.

"You worked in the Fair Play for Cuba thing?"

"Yeah."

"Do you think that the attitude of the United States towards Cuba will change now that the president's been assassinated?"

Oswald looked at Captain Fritz and said, "I believe that I've been filed on for the murder of the president. Is that right?"

"Yes, that's true," Fritz answered.

"Well, I don't think that I should elaborate on that too much because whatever I say may be construed in a different manner than which I might say it."

After announcing that he would not respond to the question, Oswald proceeded to give an answer. "In all countries, and this is no exception, if the leader dies or gets killed, there's always a second in command that takes over. In this case, I think his name is Johnson. As far as I know, Johnson's ideas is [*sic*] no different than Kennedy's, so I don't see any change in the attitude towards Cuba."[11]

At that point Fritz interrupted the interrogation. "What about this card we got out of your billfold? This draft registration card where it showed A. J. Hidell?" Oswald showed a flash of anger. "Now, I have told you all I am going to tell you about that card in my billfold. You have the card yourself, and you know as much about it as I do."[12]

Realizing they had reached a dead end, Fritz switched topics and asked Oswald about his actions that day at the school book depository. He said that at lunch time one of the "Negro" employees asked him if you would like to sit and eat lunch with him. Oswald claimed that he responded "Yes, but I can't go right now. You go ahead, but send the elevator back up." Asked about his actions after the shooting, Oswald explained: "I just went downstairs. I went down, and as I started to go out and see what it was all about, a police officer stopped me just before I got to the front door, and started to ask me some questions, and my superintendent of the place stepped up and told the officers that I am one of the employees of the building, so he told me to step aside for a little bit and we would get to you later. Then I just went out in the crowd to see what it was all about."[13]

Fritz raised Buell Wesley Frazier's claim that Oswald had carried a large brown paper wrapping with him to work that morning. Oswald denied it, saying it was just his lunch. What was the size of your lunch bag? "Oh, I don't recall, it may have been a small sack or a large sack, you don't always find one that fits your sandwich." Fritz kept pushing the subject. Frazier had said that Oswald placed the package in the back seat. Oswald claimed that he placed it on his lap in the front seat. When told of Frazier's claim, Oswald responded: "Oh, he must be mistaken, or else thinking about some other time he picked me up."[14]

When they asked him about the shooting of Officer Tippit, Oswald responded: "I don't know what you are talking about. The only thing I am in here for is because I popped a policeman in the nose in a theater on Jefferson Avenue, which I readily admit I did, because I was protecting myself."[15]

Fritz wanted to know how he got the money to pay for the trip to Mexico. Oswald said it did not cost much money — only $26 a night for the hotel. The meals were inexpensive. He said that he went to the Soviet embassy in Mexico to get permission to travel to Russia by way of Cuba. They refused his request, and told him to come back in thirty days.[16]

He was asked why he visited his wife on Thursday night when he normally visited her on the weekends. He said that on that particular weekend there was going to be a party. He did not want to be around with a house full of children at such a time. That's why he made his weekly visit on a Thursday night.[17]

Seeing the suspect for the first time, Holmes was impressed by the way he handled himself. Oswald seemed composed, he answered easy questions and deflected the tough ones. "He was not particularly obnoxious," he reflected later. "He seemed to be intelligent. He seemed to be clear minded. He seemed to have a good memory." Secret Service agent Sorrels, who had been in the room for most of the interrogation sessions over the past two days, claimed that Oswald's attitude had changed by Sunday morning. He was talking more openly. He was not giving out any information but he wasn't showing the flashes of anger and defiance that he had revealed the previous days. It's possible that the change in Oswald's attitude convinced Fritz to continue the interrogation in the hopes of getting a confession before they transferred him to the county jail.[18]

As the morning dragged on, Holmes noticed people milling around outside the office, the chief of police among them. Every once in a while they would rap on the door, or crack the door open. Holmes said they "gave all the appearance of being impatient." But Fritz told him to ignore them. "Don't worry about the man," he said. "If you got any more questions, ask him."[19]

...

Jack Ruby was woken up at 8:30 a.m. on Sunday morning by a phone call from his housekeeper. "He sounded just terribly strange to me," she recalled. He could not go back to sleep so he got up, read the morning paper, and watched the local assassination coverage on television. He sat around in his underwear until shortly after 10:00 a.m. — the time that Curry had suggested the transfer could take place. At 10:19 a.m., he received a call from one of his dancers. She needed money. He promised to drive down to the Western Union office and wire her $25, but he warned that it would "take a little while to get dressed."[20]

At 10:30 a.m., already thirty minutes past the announced transfer time, Ruby was leisurely getting ready for the day. There was no urgency to his actions. He took a shower, shaved, and lovingly combed in his Maclean's hair lotion. He put on a dark suit jacket, stuck his glasses in the pocket, and gingerly fixed atop his head a gray hat with his name stamped in gold. He picked up his dachshund, Sheba, stuck her in the back seat of his car, and told his roommate that he was going downtown. "George, I'm taking the dog down to the club.[21]

Leaving the apartment a few minutes before 11:00 a.m., he once again drove past Dealey Plaza, where a crowd gathered and new wreaths had appeared overnight. As he drove past the jail he noticed a large crowd and had assumed that Oswald had already been transferred. A series of unforeseen circumstances, however, would soon bring the two men together. [22]

CHAPTER 16:

"... You're Just Being Melodramatic"

While Postal Inspector Harry Holmes and Secret Service agent Thomas Kelley continued questioning Oswald, Captain J. W. Fritz snuck out of the room and went to have a cup of coffee with James Leavelle at the White Plaza, a local coffee shop. They were about to give up their prisoner and neither man was happy with the plans for transferring Oswald from the city hall police lockup to the better-equipped and more secure cells at the Dallas County Courthouse.

On Saturday, Chief Curry had made two critical decisions: First, he announced that the police would transfer Oswald on Sunday morning in full view of the world's media. Second, in order to make sure Oswald was kept secure during the transfer, Curry wanted to place him in the back of an armored car — a "money wagon" — for the short trip to the county jail.

Fritz and Leavelle opposed both ideas as impractical. Now they had added reason to object. During the night, both the Dallas police and the local FBI office received a call that about a hundred men were going to kidnap Oswald. According to Leavelle's account, the caller, who had specific knowledge of the transfer plan, warned "if you use that armored motor vehicle, we're going to barricade the streets and turn it over and set it on fire." Fritz preferred they use a faster, more nimble police car, which could evade or outrun a potential adversary. A "money wagon," he believed, was too easy a target: too clumsy and slow.[1]

As Leavelle and Fritz returned to the police station after their short break they ran into Curry. Fritz reiterated his objections. "Chief, if somebody . . . if they try to block the street," he said, "we can't do anything with them in that truck. But if we have . . . [Oswald] in a car, we could spin that around in the middle of the street and go in the other direction."

Curry remained reluctant to change plans, insisting that the armored car represented the safest option. Leavelle, who opposed the whole idea of transferring Oswald at a prearranged time, jumped into the conversation. "We don't owe the media anything," he said, "and I'm fed up to here with them." He suggested that they sneak Oswald out the first floor without informing the news media. Curry vetoed the idea. "I have given them my word that they can film the transfer, and I'm going to keep it because I don't want them to think that we've abused him or mistreated him in any way. And that's the best way to prove it is to let them film the transfer."[2]

By the time Fritz and Leavelle made it up to the third floor, however, the plans had changed, but not because Curry had agreed with their argument. More practical considerations won out: an air conditioning duct prevented the armored truck from squeezing into the basement. Curry had decided on an alternative plan. He would use the armored car as a decoy and transfer Oswald in an unmarked police car.[3]

At 11:00 a.m., Fritz walked back into the interrogation room for the final minutes of questioning. Sorrels asked Oswald the last question, asking why the name "A. Hidell" appeared on the New Orleans mailbox. "I never used that name," Oswald responded. Although his position remained the same, Sorrels noticed Oswald's cold reserve beginning to thaw. "I felt he was less arrogant," he told William Manchester in 1964, "more ready to break."[4]

• • •

At 11:05 a.m., Jack Ruby parked his car across the street from the Western Union station, which was only one block from police headquarters. He left his dog in the car and walked across the street. He was carrying his gun along with $2,000 in cash, which was stashed in every pocket.[5]

• • •

We will never know if Oswald was ready "to break" because Fritz officially ended the interrogation at 11:10 a.m. "We're going to move you to the county jail now," Fritz told Oswald, "It's gotten cooler outside. Would you like to have another shirt or a sweater to wear?" Oswald, seeming disinterested, shrugged, "I guess so."

Fritz asked an officer to bring Oswald some of his clothes, which were being held in a nearby room. An officer brought in some clothes off the rack and started to give Oswald a light-colored jacket or shirt. "If it's all the same to you," Oswald said, "I'd rather wear that black sweater." An officer unlocked his handcuffs so he could pull the sweater over his head. "Would you care to put on a hat?" Fritz asked. "They'll be a lot of TV cameras and photographers in the basement. Everybody has seen you bareheaded. Maybe you'd like a hat to disguise you?" Once again, Oswald rejected an opportunity to hide from the media. "I don't have anything to hide," he said.[6]

Fritz asked one of the officers for the time. It was 11:15 a.m. "Call the jail office," he said. "Tell them we'll be down in five minutes."[7]

• • •

Jack Ruby walked into the Western Union just as Lee Harvey Oswald was putting on his sweater in Captain Fritz's office. According to the clerk, Ruby was not in a hurry. Since there was no television or radio at the Western Union office he would not have known whether the transfer had taken place or not. The cost of sending the moneygram was $26.87. Ruby gave the clerk $30 and waited for his change. The clerk copied the information and then handed Ruby a receipt stamped: 1963 Nov 24 a.m. 11 17.[8]

When he walked out to his car, Ruby noticed a crowd outside the police department. A man who always needed to be near the center of the action, Ruby strolled down the street to see what was happening.[9]

• • •

As Fritz prepared to leave with Oswald a Secret Service agent approached him. "If I were you, I would not move Oswald to the county jail at an announced time like this," he said. "I would take him out at three or four in the morning when there's no one around." Personally Fritz could not agree more. But this was not his show. "Chief Curry wants to go along with the press and not try to put anything over on them." Fritz told him.

In Captain Fritz's office, Oswald stood quietly, his hands manacled in front. Fearing that someone might try to kidnap Oswald, Fritz had him handcuffed to Detective Leavelle. "Cap figured somebody ought to be handcuffed to him," Leavelle recalled, "so if they took him, they had to take me, too, and it wouldn't be that easy."[10]

Leavelle, who was wearing a pale gray Stetson and his only Neiman Marcus suit, snapped one end of a second pair of handcuffs on Oswald's right wrist, the other end on his own left wrist. "Lee, if anybody shoots at you, I hope they're as good a shot as you are," Leavelle said, trying to add some humor to a very tense atmosphere. "Aw, there ain't going to be anybody shooting at me," Oswald replied with a laugh, "you're just being melodramatic."[11]

CHAPTER 17:

"You Killed My President, You Rat Son of a Bitch!"

At 11:15 am, with Captain Fritz and Lieutenant Swain leading the way, Oswald and Detective Leavelle, along with detectives L.C. Graves and L.D. Montgomery, left the office and started walking to the elevator that would take them to the basement. Most reporters had moved their equipment down to the basement for the transfer, but Ike Pappas hoped to get an exclusive with Oswald as he was being escorted to the elevator. "Do you have anything to say in your defense?" he shouted to Oswald. "I want to see the American Civil Liberties Union," Oswald muttered before detectives pushed Pappas to the side and stepped onto the elevator. They would be the last words that Lee Harvey Oswald would speak.[1]

"Oswald was very calm," recalled detective Graves. "We didn't ask him anything, and he didn't volunteer anything. We just told him we were transferring him to the county and that was it." When the elevator opened in the basement, they walked approximately thirty feet to the jailhouse door. They hesitated inside the door waiting for an "all clear sign," indicating that the garage was safe for them to enter.[2]

...

It took Ruby about ninety seconds to walk the 350 feet from the Western Union office on Main Street to City Hall. He arrived at 11:20 a.m. As he approached the basement garage, the policeman who had been guarding the twelve-foot-wide entrance ramp momentarily stepped into the street to direct traffic, allowing Ruby to slip down the ramp without breaking stride. Just as he reached the basement where reporters were lined up he heard a cry: "Here he comes!"[3]

• • •

At 11:21 a.m., Oswald entered the underground garage surrounded by a phalanx of police officers. Detective Graves had assumed that the garage would be cleared of everyone except journalists and police officers. "We were told that the way would be open and nobody would be interfering with us. Wouldn't be anybody there. All we would have to do was walk to the car." Instead, they were confronted by a chaotic scene. Leavelle estimated there were about 150 people, mainly newsmen and police officers, crammed into the basement.[4]

The flash bulbs and bright television camera lights would have at least temporarily blinded Oswald as he entered the garage. He walked about ten feet into the basement before hesitating. The white sedan that was supposed to be parked about thirteen to fourteen feet just outside the door was still rolling back, struggling to get into position against the tide of reporters who surged toward Oswald. The driver blasted the horn as Captain Fritz reached for the back-door handle.

Ike Pappas, who had just interviewed Oswald on the third floor, had enough time to run down the stairs and get into the basement before the elevator arrived. He maneuvered his way to the front of the line. When Oswald appeared, Pappas pushed close to him again, thrust his microphone in his face and asked: "Do you have anything to say in your defense?"[5]

Before Oswald could answer, Jack Ruby lunged from the crowd to Oswald's left front, his arm outstretched with a gun in his right hand. Ruby yelled, "You killed my president, you rat son of a bitch!" and pulled the trigger.[6]

It took Ruby fewer than two seconds to step from the crowd and fire. There was no time for anyone to react. "I had Oswald by the belt in addition to being handcuffed to him," Leavelle recalled, "and I tried to jerk him behind me but all I succeeded in doing was turning his body a little bit so that instead of hitting him dead center, it hit him about four inches to the left of the navel." The result was that instead of a direct shot to the stomach, the bullet entered on the left side and crossed diagonally, hitting every major organ in his abdomen.[7]

There was a moment of silence, a split second, before Oswald let out a cry and grabbed his stomach, his face contorted in pain.

Detective Graves grabbed Ruby's arm by the wrist with his left hand and reached for the gun with his right hand. Ruby was still flexing his fingers trying to pull the trigger, but Graves had his fingers on the hammer of the gun, preventing it from shooting. "Turn it loose," he kept shouting to Ruby. Eventually he twisted the gun out of his hand. At the same time, Detective Montgomery grabbed Ruby around the throat and was applying a choke hold on him. Ruby was not giving up easily. "He was putting up a struggle," Montgomery recalled.[8]

Leavelle and Detective Billy Combest picked Oswald up by the arms and legs, carried him back into the jail office, and laid him down. Combest unlocked the handcuffs. Someone shouted, "Get a doctor!"[9]

Oswald was moaning as they took off the handcuffs. Leavelle pulled up Oswald's sweater and saw a bullet hole in the lower left part of his stomach, the flesh around it bruised and purple.

Oswald continued to moan and seemed conscious. "Is there anything you want to tell me?" Detective Combest asked him. "Is there anything you want to say right now before it's too late?" Oswald's eyes were open. He appeared to recognize that the detective was speaking to him. "Do you have anything you want to tell us now?" the detective asked again. Oswald shook his head slightly, as if to say, "No."

Oswald's shooting marked the first time in American history that a homicide had occurred in front of live television cameras. Before then, it had been a quiet morning with most networks focused on religious services and the plans for President Kennedy's funeral. NBC telecast the dramatic events live. CBS was on the air in less than a minute after the shooting occurred. NBC reporter Tom Pettit described the scene in the parking garage. "He's been shot! He's been shot! Lee Oswald has been shot. There is absolute panic. Pandemonium has broken out." Commentators point out that whoever shot Oswald was well dressed, wearing a brown coat. Given the tight security, there was some question about whether it might have been a detective who pulled the trigger.[10]

•••

At the time of the shooting the nation's attention had been focused on the North Portico of the White House. A military guard was preparing to transfer President Kennedy's casket from the East Room of the White House to the Capitol Rotunda, where he would remain until the funeral the following day.

Inside the White House, Mrs. Kennedy and Robert F. Kennedy were kneeling before the open coffin, saying their final goodbye to the slain president. Mrs. Kennedy placed notes from Caroline and John, along with her own letter and a few mementos that were meaningful to the president — gold cufflinks and a presidential seal crafted into a whalebone — next to her husband. Robert Kennedy took an engraved silver rosary from his pocket and placed it in the coffin.[11]

Outside, a crowd of three hundred thousand people stood under the bright sun lining the two-mile route from the White House to the Capitol. Those who had transistor radios spread the word of the shooting of Lee Harvey Oswald in Dallas.

CHAPTER 18:

"I Hope I Killed the Son of a Bitch"

A twenty-five-year-old medical student at Southwestern medical school named Frederick A. Bieberdorf made his way into the jail office where he found Jack Ruby and Lee Harvey Oswald lying faceup a few feet apart. Bieberdorf happened to be working that day providing first aid to the inmates at the jail.

The medical student rushed to Oswald's side. His initial impression was that Oswald was already dead. The prisoner's pupils were slightly dilated, and Bieberdorf could detect no pulse or any breathing. He also could not hear heartbeats, but that could have been because of all the noise in the room. One of the detectives had lifted Oswald's shirt up to his chest, exposing a "puncture wound" on the left side of his stomach just below the rib cage. Oddly, there was no blood. Oswald had sustained a massive wound but all the bleeding was internal. The medical student noticed that there was no exit wound. He could feel the bullet just under the skin on the right side of Oswald's rib cage, which meant that the bullet had traversed the entire abdomen and likely had hit a number of major organs.

Although Oswald had sustained a stomach wound, Bieberdorf started massaging Oswald's sternum in an effort to get a heartbeat. Secret Service agent Forest Sorrels, who raced down from the third floor when he heard Oswald had been shot, found Bieberdorf kneeling between Oswald's legs "giving him artificial respiration." All the medical student managed to do was to pump more blood out of Oswald's body. William Manchester, noting that this procedure was "the worst thing" for a stomach wound, concluded: "Dallas police were Keystone cops to the last." Bieberdorf spent about five minutes with Oswald before the ambulance arrived.[1]

Lying a few feet away was Oswald's assassin, Jack Ruby. After subduing him, police had dragged Ruby back into the jail office and laid him down on the floor. Ruby was hollering, "You all know me. I'm Jack Ruby." He could not understand why the police were being so rough. He thought he had done them a favor. "I hope I killed the son of a bitch," Ruby shouted. "I intended to shoot him three times. . . . You didn't think I was going to let him get by with it, did you?"

As he continued his protest, officers picked Ruby up and placed him on the elevator. "Somebody had to do it, you guys couldn't," he told officers as they escorted him to the third-floor interrogation room — the same room that Oswald had occupied for much of the past forty-eight hours.[2]

While the police removed Ruby, the ambulance attendants arrived and placed Oswald's limp body on a stretcher and carried him out to the parking lot, his left arm dragging on the floor as they walked, and placed him in the ambulance. Two detectives jumped into the rear seat of the ambulance. Detective Leavelle remained by Oswald's side during the trip to the hospital.[3]

As the ambulance sped down Henry Hines Boulevard toward Parkland Hospital, Bieberdorf placed an oxygen cup over Oswald's nose and continued to massage the sternum. Oswald remained unconscious the entire trip. Five blocks from the hospital, however, he suddenly started thrashing about, resisting Bieberdorf's efforts to massage his chest and pulling at the resuscitator cup over his mouth. Lee Harvey Oswald was still alive.[4]

The ambulance pulled into the hospital's emergency entrance, the same one used for President Kennedy two days earlier. Oswald arrived just as Nellie Connally was walking into the hospital to visit her ailing husband. A police contingent was already in place to assist the ambulance driver as he backed up to the entrance. Attendants quickly unloaded Oswald and wheeled him into the hospital.

A hospital administrator, who considered it sacrilege to treat Oswald in the same emergency room as JFK, steered them into trauma room two, across the hall.[5]

Doctors Malcolm Perry and Ronald Jones, who had worked to save the president's life on Friday, rushed down to see Oswald. Perry observed that Oswald "was quite seriously injured." He was blue from lack of oxygen, and he was attempting to breathe but clearly having difficulty. Perry examined his chest and noticed the entrance point of the bullet wound on the left side. He could feel the bullet just under the skin.

Detective Leavelle remained by Oswald's side even as the doctors started working on him. "I want that bullet," he told them. The doctor took a scalpel and slit open the skin. The bullet popped out like a "ripe grape." Leavelle handed the nurse a pocketknife and told her to etch her initials on the bullet "so you can identify that as [the] one coming out of him." He wrapped the initialed bullet in tissue and put it in his pocket.[6]

The emergency team had already started resuscitation routines designed to stabilize the patient. They made three small incisions on Oswald's legs and his left forearm to induce fluids. They inserted a chest tube to prevent the left lung from collapsing. They also lowered the front of the gurney to help get blood to Oswald's heart and brain.

Having stabilized their patient, doctors rushed him into the express elevator, which took him to the operating suites on the second floor. Within twelve minutes after entering the hospital Oswald had been delivered to the operating room and prepared for surgery.

Journalists were trying to make sense of the events on live television as cameras captured images of the chaos and confusion. NBC's Tom Pettit reported that the shooter was a man known locally who owned a gambling casino in Dallas. He pointed out that whoever shot Oswald apparently had no difficulty entering a highly secured area. At 11:42 a.m., about eighteen minutes after the shooting, Frank McGee named Oswald's shooter as "Jack Ruby" or "Jack Lobe." By this point, NBC had switched back to Washington and was providing audio from Dallas, reporting that Oswald was in critical condition. According to a witness, Oswald's head was "bobbing" back and forth as he was carried into the hospital.[7]

...

In the operating room, doctors began working frantically to save Oswald's life. They faced a daunting task: The bullet had ruptured the aorta, the main blood vessel from the heart, and the vena cava below the diaphragm. The bullet also ripped through the spleen, the pancreas, the right kidney and the right lobe of the liver. The bullet had stopped at the right chest wall.

Dr. Perry found the source of most of the bleeding, the ruptured aorta, and used his fingers to clamp it, while other doctors managed to stop the bleeding from another main artery. Working at a breakneck pace for the next hour, the surgical team stopped all the major bleeding and restored Oswald's blood pressure to 100/85. They began to think they may be able to save their patient's life. "The fact is we were very close, I think, to winning the battle," reflected Dr. Perry. While acknowledging that patients with injuries of this magnitude rarely survived, Perry felt that "once we controlled the hemorrhage and once I had control of the aorta and was able to stop the bleeding of that area I actually felt we had a very good chance . . . " of saving him.[8]

Suddenly, Dr. Jenkins reported Oswald's heart was weakening. His pulse rate dropped from 85 to 40, then seconds later to zero. The tremendous blood loss had set the stage for irreversible shock and cardiac arrest. Dr. Perry grabbed a knife, opened the left side of Oswald's chest, and massaged the heart. He managed to obtain a palpable pulse in the blood vessels feeding the neck and head, but he was unable to get the heart to pump on its own. They hit Oswald with 240, 360, 500, and finally 700 volts of electricity, but still no heartbeat. Dr. Perry stitched a pacemaker into the right ventricle of the heart, hoping to artificially induce the heart to pump. The pacemaker created a feeble muscle reaction but no effective heartbeat.

After a frenzied struggle, Dr. Perry called a halt. Oswald's pupils were fixed and dilated, there was no blood flow, no respiratory effort, and no effective pulse. Lee Harvey Oswald was dead. It was seven minutes after one o'clock, almost exactly forty-eight hours after Kennedy expired.

• • •

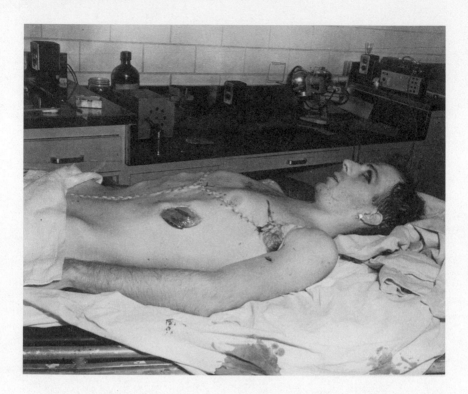

Ruby was very talkative and excited. "If I had planned this I couldn't have had my timing better," he said. "It was one chance in one million." He claimed that he wanted to get off at least three shots, but was tackled after getting off only one. When asked why he shot Oswald, Ruby replied that he did not want Mrs. Kennedy to have to return to Dallas for trial and "go through this ordeal for this son of a bitch." Secret Service agent Sorrels asked one question upon entering the room: "Jack — why?" Ruby replied: "I guess I just had to show the world that a Jew has guts."[9]

Assistant District Attorney Alexander, who also went to see Ruby and who would later prosecute him for Oswald's murder, was convinced that the nightclub owner never expected to spend the night in jail. "God-damn it, Jack, what did you do this for?" Alexander asked him. "Well you guys couldn't do it. Someone had to do it. That son of a bitch killed my president." Alexander believed that Ruby "thought he was going to go through the booking, and then he would be released. He just thought, how mad can you get with the guy who just killed the president's assassin? Jack

actually thought he might come out of this as a hero of sorts, getting the acknowledgment he always wanted in Dallas. He thought he had erased any stigma the city had by knocking off Oswald."[10]

EPILOGUE

On Monday, November 25, while kings and queens gathered in Washington to bid farewell to a fallen leader, members of the Oswald family gathered in a remote corner of Rose Hill Cemetery in Fort Worth, Texas.

Shortly after 4:00 p.m., Oswald was buried in a plain, cloth-covered wooden coffin. Attending the service were his widow, his mother, his two baby daughters, and brother Robert. "We are not here to judge," said the Rev. Louis Saunders. "We are here to lay him away before an understanding God." There were no pallbearers. Reporters covering the funeral volunteered to carry the coffin. Oswald had no friends.[1]

Before the coffin was lowered into the ground, Marina removed the cover and lifted her two children to view the body. "Look, Poppa sleeps," she said to them in Russian. She and Oswald's mother kissed the accused assassin. Marina then placed her wedding ring on her husband's left finger. The coffin was then enclosed in a vault adorned with a few red and white chrysanthemums, and then lowered into the ground. As the coffin descended into the vault they each threw a handful of dirt on the casket. The entire ceremony lasted twenty minutes.[2]

...

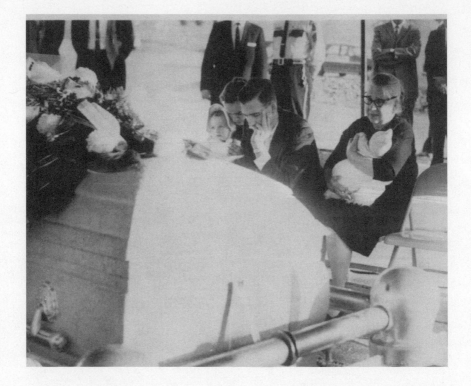

Oswald remained an elusive figure, even to those who were with him for the last forty-eight hours of his life. FBI agents Bookhout and Hosty expressed contempt for Oswald, whom they dismissed as "arrogant and argumentative." Their frustration was understandable. They were angry that Oswald appeared so nonchalant, so cocky, especially in the face of such an awful crime.[3]

Two Dallas detectives formed a very different impression. Richard Sims and Elmer Boyd flanked Oswald throughout the interrogation sessions. They never said a word, but they observed Oswald for two days. They were both impressed by their prisoner's general demeanor. According to Sims, Oswald "conducted himself . . . better than anyone I have ever seen during interrogation. He was calm and wasn't nervous." He seemed to be in complete control.[4]

Boyd reflected years later that he had never met another man like Oswald. He was in Boyd's opinion very intelligent and efficient at anticipating questions before they were asked. "[J]ust as soon as you ask him a question, he would just give you the answer right back — he didn't hesitate about his answers." Boyd told the Warren Commission: "I never saw a man that could answer questions like he did." In a word, Boyd summarized Oswald's behavior as "cool."[5]

Oswald gave Detective James Leavelle the impression "of being a man with a lot better education than his formal education indicated." He was convinced that Oswald maintained control the entire time. "In fact, he struck me as a man who enjoyed the situation immensely and was enjoying the publicity and everything was coming his way."[6]

To Captain Fritz, who spent more time with Oswald after the shooting than anyone else, Oswald was too good — too skilled at anticipating questions; too quick to deflect probing inquiries; too calm in the face of overwhelming circumstances; and too fearless considering the charges against him. "I know a lot of people call him a nut all the time but he didn't talk like a nut," he told the Warren Commission. Oswald knew exactly when to talk and when to stop. He would talk freely about topics that were not directly related to the shooting of either JFK or Officer Tippit, but as soon as Fritz asked a question that could possibly provide incriminating evidence, Oswald stopped talking. Fritz wondered: Had Oswald received special training in how to deflect police questioning?

Fritz was convinced of Oswald's guilt by the overwhelming physical evidence the police had gathered in those first forty-eight hours. But there were always questions: Had he acted alone?

• • •

Oswald's death meant that those questions would never be adequately answered. In fact, Oswald's death guaranteed that conspiracy theories would flourish. According to the *New York Times* one of the questions on the minds of many Americans in the hours after the shooting was: "Did Oswald really do it alone, or was this guy [Ruby] an accomplice who shot Oswald so he'd keep quiet?" A Maryland woman told the *Dallas Morning News*: "We may never really know the truth now." "Way I see it," said a local Dallas man, "that man (who shot Oswald) either hated him so bad that he had to shoot him, or he didn't want him to talk."[7]

The conspiracy theories quickly spread across the globe. The reaction of a French television announcer captured the sentiment of many foreign observers: "There will always be a doubt in the world whether he (Oswald) was innocent or guilty." Tass, the official Soviet news agency, said of Oswald's death: "The murderers of President John Kennedy are trying to cover-up their traces."[8]

The questions about a larger conspiracy seeped into the White House. Historian and presidential advisor Arthur Schlesinger received a call on Sunday afternoon from labor leader Walter Reuther, who suggested that the radical right had picked Oswald to do their dirty work, hoping that the communist would be held responsible. Now, he suggested, "they" killed Oswald to get him "out of the way lest he break down and talk."[9]

Most members of the presidential party who left Dallas forty-eight hours earlier paid little attention to Oswald's shooting, or the unfolding conspiracy theories. Larry O'Brien, who had helped carry the president's coffin onto *Air Force One,* said he was "no more interested than if someone had been telling me the score of a ballgame."[10]

Many White House officials, however, understood the implications of Oswald's death. General Maxwell Taylor, the chairman of the Joint Chiefs of Staff, considered how the images of "lawlessness was damaging our worldwide reputation." Reflecting later, he also felt "that there would be suspicion that the killing of Oswald by Ruby had been done to suppress something."[11]

A few minutes after the shooting, President Johnson, who was on his way back to the White House from services at St. Mark's Episcopal Church, received an urgent call from Secretary of State Dean Rusk. The secretary informed him that Oswald had been shot live "on television." Both Johnson and Rusk feared that the situation in Dallas was tarnishing America's image around the world. LBJ had been trying to allow local officials to handle the investigation, but now he believed it was time for the Justice Department and the FBI to assume complete control. Johnson approached Robert Kennedy, who at this point did not even know that Oswald had been shot, and said, "We've got to do something, we've got to do something. We've got to get involved. It's giving the United States a bad name around the world." Afterwards, Kennedy remembered that "I thought at the time that . . . [this] wasn't, it couldn't be, the thing foremost in my mind."[12]

The Secret Service, the CIA, and J. Edgar Hoover's FBI all assumed there was a link between Jack Ruby and Oswald. Dallas Secret Service agent Forrest Sorrels, who had spent the past two days interrogating Oswald, received a phone call from Secret Service head Jerry Behn in Washington. "It's a plot," Behn insisted. "Of course," Sorrels responded.[13]

• • •

On September 24, 1964, only ten months after the events in Dallas, the President's Commission on the Assassination of President Kennedy, popularly known as the Warren Commission, issued its exhaustive report, which included an 888-page summary, twenty-six volumes of supporting documents, testimony or depositions of 552 witnesses, and more than 3,100 exhibits. The commission concluded that Lee Harvey Oswald had acted alone, and from his perch on the sixth floor of the school book depository building, had fired three shots at the president. The commission found no link between Oswald and Ruby.

The report did little to stem the tide of skepticism, however. In 1966, three years after Kennedy's death, 46 percent of people surveyed believed the assassination was part of a broader plot. A *Newsweek* poll taken in 1983 on the twentieth anniversary of the assassination showed that 74 percent of Americans believed that "others were involved." In 2003, an ABC News poll revealed that only 32 percent of adults accepted the Warren Commission findings. The survey found that 70 percent believed the assassination was part of a conspiracy; 51 percent thought a second gunman was involved, and more than two-thirds suspected a government cover-up.

Skeptics charged that in a "rush to judgment" the Warren Commission ignored witnesses who claimed to hear more than three shots, and repressed evidence that could have implicated other groups with a motive to shoot the president. Such suspicions gained a new lease on life in 1992 with the release of the Hollywood film *JFK,* directed by Oliver Stone. The film portrayed an elaborate web of conspiracy involving Vice President Johnson, the FBI, the CIA, the Pentagon, defense contractors, and assorted other officials and agencies. More recent revelations about the Kennedy administration's previously secret plans to remove Castro, and the tawdry characters involved in the plots, have added fuel to these con-spiracy theories.

Many conspiracy theories are based on the belief that there were multi-ple shooters in Dealey Plaza on November 22, which provides lots of room to speculate about groups and individuals that might have been involved in the assassination. While some writers continue to cling to the multiple-shooter theory, new analysis of the forensic evidence leaves little doubt that all the bullets fired came from the sixth floor of the school book depository. Removing the other shooters leaves Lee Harvey Oswald. The only route left to maintain that JFK was killed by conspiracy of sinister forces is to repack-age Oswald, transforming a low-life loser into an American James Bond.[14]

In many of these accounts, Oswald is simply a "trigger man," or, as he would later refer to himself after his capture, "a patsy." They describe a skilled, highly trained, CIA assassin who was leading a double life as a pro-Castro militant in an effort to infiltrate and weaken Cuba's intelligence operation. Oswald, they argue, was in fact part of a nefarious alliance of right-wing intelligence officials, virulently anti-Castro groups, and self-serving mob bosses. [15]

These conspiracy theories fill in the holes in Oswald's life with the most sinister of motives: Why would the marines tolerate his open embrace of communism? (He was actually recruited by American intelligence and was being given special favors by mysterious forces in the American intelligence community. He was building his cover and the marines were, apparently, ordered to look the other way). How could he afford to defect to the Soviet Union? (U.S. intelligence provided him with the money). They claim, despite evidence to the contrary, that Oswald had "special" privileges while living in the Soviet Union. (Why? Because he provided them with the infor-mation the Soviets used to shoot down the U-2 spy plane flown by Francis Gary Powers.) If Oswald was so pro-Castro, why did he associate with so many people who were so virulently anti-communist? (He was not a Marx-ist at all; he only pretended to support the Cuban revolution in order to infiltrate pro-Castro groups in the United States for the CIA).

Most surprisingly, not only were Oswald, and the right-wing political activists he associated with, provocateurs, they were also gay. Conspiracy author Michael Kurtz asserted that "Oswald was well known among the

Cuban exile community in New Orleans both as a provocateur for the CIA and as a homosexual." He argues that Oswald traveled to New Orleans in April, 1963 not to seek employment, but to work as a secret agent inside pro-Castro groups. It was here that he conspired with his gay companions, Clay L. Shaw and David Ferrie, to undertake clandestine CIA missions. (Shaw and Clay were also the central characters in New Orleans district attorney Jim Garrison's discredited 1967 investigations made popular in Oliver Stone's hit movie, *JFK*.)[16]

The theories that Oswald was a double agent working for American intelligence fall apart when held up to the light of evidence (as well as common sense). Accepting them requires dismissing the accounts of those who knew Oswald best (including his wife), and accepting the accounts of far less credible figures. It requires substituting wild speculation for stubborn facts. The double-agent theory assumes that every twist turn in the life of this misguided, confused young man was guided by some master plan hatched in the secret recesses of the CIA. Every minor discrepancy in the public record becomes proof of a vast conspiracy. Contradictory reports about Oswald's height must mean that there were "multiple" Oswalds. The "real" Oswald was likely "switched" and replaced by an American intelligence agent, perhaps during his stint in the Marine Corps. The "new" Oswald went on to shoot JFK; the "real" one was sent to the witness protection program "or was either held prisoner or killed." Of course the "new" Oswald was so convincing that not even his own mother noticed the difference![17]

While conspiracy theorists have painted a distorted, barely recognizable, portrait of Lee Harvey Oswald, they do offer a necessary corrective to the standard, lone-gunman interpretation. It seems likely that Oswald was indeed motivated by politics — just not the right-wing politics they suggest. In understanding Oswald's motives, all roads run through Cuba. The unanswered question is whether those roads were solely a figment of Oswald's imagination, a byproduct of his inflated ego and tenuous relationship with reality, or whether Cuban intelligence officials egged on his delusions.

The most revealing and controversial evidence of some tangible Cuban connection focus on Oswald's trip to Mexico City between September 27 and October 2, 1963. According to some sources, during his visit to the Cuban embassy Oswald threatened to kill "that son of a bitch" John

Kennedy. The most credible source to make this claim was Jack Childs, an undercover FBI agent who managed to earn the trust of Fidel Castro. Childs and Castro had met in Moscow in May 1963 and developed a close rapport. In 1964, the FBI sent Childs to Havana to talk with Castro about the assassination. Believing that he was speaking to a confidant, Castro told him that Oswald had become agitated when he visited the Cuban embassy in Mexico City weeks before Kennedy's assassination. Fidel told him that Oswald "[s]tormed into the embassy, demanded the visa and when it was refused to him headed out saying, 'I'm going to kill Kennedy for this.'" J. Edgar Hoover forwarded the story to the Warren Commission, but the investigators for some reason chose to ignore it.[18]

In 2012, Brian Latell, the CIA's former national intelligence officer for Latin America, revealed that a former Castro aide told U.S. intelligence a similar story. "Our people in Mexico gave us the details in a full report of how he acted when he came to our embassy," the defector quoted Castro as saying. And, Castro confessed, Oswald had indeed threatened Kennedy's life.[19]

Latell, however, takes the story a step further. He argues that Cuban intelligence encouraged Oswald to carry out the threat. "There is a very good chance that the Cuban intelligence officers at the consulate encouraged Oswald to kill Kennedy, and they could have done it without Castro even knowing it," he reflected. As proof, Latell cites the statements of Vladimir Rodriguez Lahera, nicknamed "Laddie," who defected to the United States in 1964. Laddie claimed Oswald maintained contacts with Cuban intelligence officers after leaving Mexico City. "Laddie believed there had been sustained Cuban engagement with Oswald," Latell wrote.

Critics have raised a number of appropriate questions about these accounts. Two of the witnesses to Oswald's Mexico City temper tantrum had no recollection of him threatening Kennedy's life. The 1978 House Select Committee on Assassinations (HSCA) investigated the claims, interviewed many of the witnesses, reviewed the evidence, and concluded Oswald had made no such threat. As Vincent Bugliosi stated: "The story doesn't make sense. *Why would Oswald threaten to kill Kennedy because the Cuban consulate turned down his request for a visa?*" Also, Castro maintained tight control of his intelligence operations. Would he have allowed such a risky venture to escape his purview?[20]

The HSCA, however, did not have access to the information from Cuban defectors upon which Latell based his account. The connection between being denied a visa by the Cuban government and killing the president of the United States may not be immediately evident, but in Oswald's twisted mind it may have all made sense. There was no way a local bureaucrat in Mexico City could refuse to provide him with a visa if he assassinated the president of the United States.

Latell also tells the story of Major Florentino Aspillaga, a high-level Cuban spy who defected to the United States in 1987. In 1963, Aspillaga was in Havana and had been monitoring Miami radio communications from the CIA headquarters in Langley, Virginia, and from the Cuban exile community in Miami. On November 22, 1963, sometime between 9:00 a.m. and 9:30 a.m., Aspillaga received a coded message telling him to use a secure phone to call headquarters. His superiors told him to redirect his powerful antennas "from Langley and Miami toward Texas." He was instructed to listen and then report "if anything important occurs." He later told the CIA: "They knew Kennedy would be killed . . . Fidel knew."[21]

Latell, who debriefed Aspillaga for the CIA, wrote in his 2012 book, *Castro's Secrets,* "I had come to believe that he was telling the unvarnished truth." In response to critics who claim that Aspillaga's memory cannot be trusted, Lattell told me that the defector "was vetted for years by the FBI and the CIA and he was never known to have embellished, exaggerated, or prevaricated. Why would he start lying to me?" In revealing this information, Aspillaga made a critical distinction between Castro having prior knowledge of the assassination and having somehow been involved in ordering it. He had no evidence to suggest that Castro plotted the murder.

While the new evidence stops far short of proving Castro's involvement in the assassination, it does raise troubling questions. Would Cuban intelligence have been familiar enough with Oswald to know that he lived in Dallas, and that the city would be the likely setting for an assassination? Latell believes the most likely scenario was that the day before the assassination, when he realized that Kennedy's motorcade would pass by his window, Oswald called Silvia Duran, the official at the Cuban consulate with whom he had dealt. (Duran's phone number was found in Oswald's address book). He could have said something along the lines of: "Remember what I said I was going to do? I'm going to have an opportunity tomorrow morning. Stay tuned." There is, however, no evidence that Oswald made any such call.[22]

The possibility that Cuban intelligence encouraged Oswald to kill Kennedy is tantalizing, but still unproven. Oswald could just as easily have been provoked to kill Kennedy by news stories and magazine articles published in the days and weeks before the assassination which discussed the president's plans to step up pressure on Castro, and the Cuban leader's fears of U.S.-sponsored assassination plots. Left-wing periodicals, which Oswald was known to have read, included articles detailing Castro's fears that Kennedy was trying to "tighten the noose around Cuba."

But the new information does reinforce a possible political motive to the assassination, highlighting that Oswald was driven by a desire — potentially stoked by Cuban intelligence — to prove his fidelity to the revolution, gain Castro's respect, and possibly travel to Cuba as a conquering hero. In his fantasy world, Oswald probably assumed that he would be welcomed in Havana as the man who killed the American devil, not appreciating that neither Castro nor the Soviets would wish to incur the wrath of the United States by harboring JFK's assassin.

• • •

These insights may also may explain Oswald's actions after the shooting. Was he trying to get a bus back to Mexico where he could receive his imagined reward? Ironically, although he did not know it, the Cubans had in fact granted him a transit visa to Havana just hours before he shot JFK. From there he could have gone on to the Soviet Union. Had he not encountered officer Tippit, it is possible that Oswald would have made it to Mexico City.

Oswald's actions in the final forty-eight hours of his life offer no conclusive answers to these questions, but a few highly speculative observations are possible. While the argument that Oswald was a double agent defy reason, it is also hard to accept that Oswald killed Kennedy for the attention. When the Warren Commission asked Marina Oswald what her husband's motive had been, she responded: "I can conclude that he wanted in any way, whether good or bad, to do something that would make him outstanding, that he would be known in history." But if Oswald shot Kennedy for the attention and fame, why did he not wear it as a badge of honor? Why did he spend two days denying any knowledge of the assassination? It's possible that he was laying the groundwork for a sensational murder trial that would keep him in the news for months and provide a forum to share his political views with the world. If that were the case, why did he even try to escape?

The time between the assassination of JFK and the shooting of Officer Tippit is critical to understanding Oswald's mindset. Where was he going when he fled the book depository? Some scholars of the assassination have argued that Oswald never expected to get out of the book depository without being caught and had no clear plan of escape. More plausible is the argument that Oswald planned to get out of the country and back to Mexico. He was only a few blocks away from a bus route that would have, with connections, taken him over the border. Yet, if his plan was to go to Mexico, why would he leave all of his money for Marina? He also did not have a visa to cross the border.

If the assumption is that Oswald planned to get to Mexico City then it becomes a realistic possibility that he had some assistance. His skill in parrying with Fritz, and every other law enforcement officer who participated in the interrogation, reveals that Oswald was bright, paid attention to details, and certainly possessed the mental agility to plan an escape route. If so, he would have known that he needed money to survive and a visa to get across the border. If his plan was to get out of the country, it is just as likely that he believed that he did not need money or a visa because he expected that someone was going to help him.

The question that still needs to be answered is whether the expectation of assistance was simply a product of Oswald's imagination — the outgrowth of the fantasy he had created in his mind that Castro would come to his rescue. Or, had Cuban intelligence, perhaps freelancing, encouraged him to expect help getting across the border? And, what was the nature of that encouragement — did it consist of empty promises or were there tangible assets in place to get Oswald out of the United States? Recent revelations have offered tantalizing hints, yet no definitive proof, of Cuban involvement in the assassination. Fifty years later many questions remain unanswered.

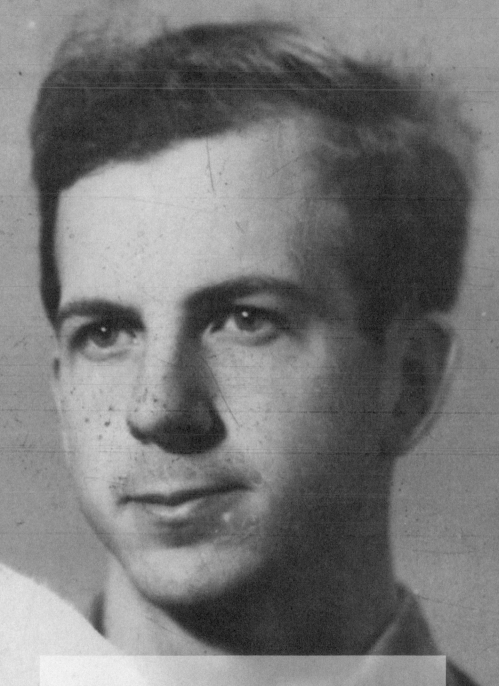

LEE HARVEY OSWALD:
A TIMELINE OF HIS FINAL HOURS

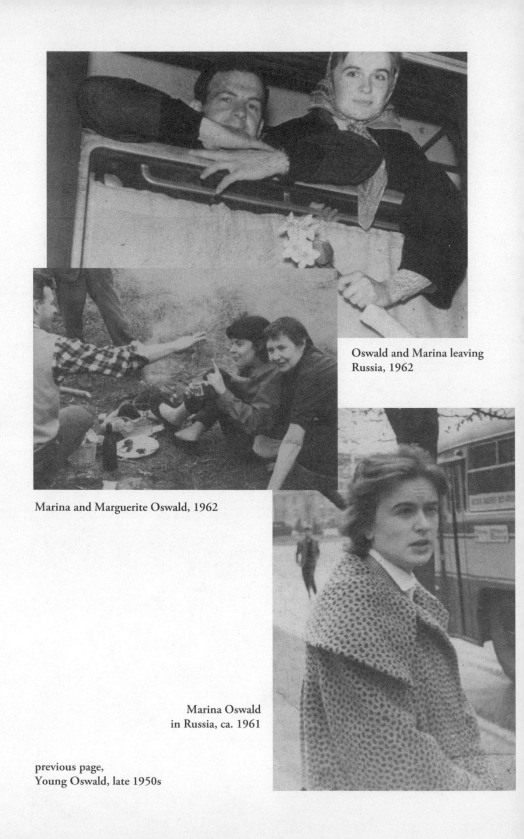

Oswald and Marina leaving
Russia, 1962

Marina and Marguerite Oswald, 1962

Marina Oswald
in Russia, ca. 1961

previous page,
Young Oswald, late 1950s

Personal photo of LHO, early 1960s

FROM: LEE H. OSWALD, P.O. BOX 6225, DALLAS, TEXAS
MARINA NICHILAYEVA OSWALD, SOVIET CITIZEN

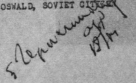

TO: CONSULAR DIVISION
EMBASSY U.S.S.R.
WASHINGTON, D.C.
NOV. 9, 1963

Dear sirs;

This is to inform you of recent events since my meetings with comrade Kostin in the Embassy Of the Soviet Union, Mexico City, Mexico.

I was unable to remain in Mexico indefinily because of my mexican visa restrictions which was for 15 days only. I could not take a chance on reqesting a new visa unless I used my real name, so I retured to the United States.

I had not planned to contact the Soviet embassy in Mexico so they were unprepared, had I been able to reach the Soviet Embassy in Havana as planned, the embassy there would have had time to complete our business.

Of corse the Soviet embassy was not at fault, they were, as I say unprepared, the Cuban consulate was guilty of a gross breach of regulations, I am glad he has since been replced.

The Federal Bureu of Investigation is not now interested in my activities in the progressive organization" Fair Play For Cuba Committee", of which I was secretary in New Orleans(state Louisiana) since I no longer reside in that state. However, the F.B.I. has visted us here in Dallas,Texas, on November 1st. Agent James P. Hasty warned me that if I engaged in F.P.C.C. activities in Texas the F.B.I. will again take an"interrest" in me.

This agent also "suggested" to Marina Nichilayeva that she could remain in the United States under F.B.I. "proteotion", that is , she could defect from the Soviet Uion ,of couse, I and my wife strongly protested these tactics by the notorious F.B.I..

Please inform us of the arrival of our Soviet entrance visa's as soon as they come.

Also, this is to inform you of the birth,on October 20 , 1963 of a DAUGHTER, AUDREY MARINA OSWALD in DALLAS,TEXAS, to my wife.

Respectfully,

FRIDAY, NOVEMBER 22, 1963

12:30 P.M. President John F. Kennedy is assassinated in Dealey Plaza, Dallas, Texas.

JFK motorcade

Polaroid of JFK limousine speeding off after shots

12:31 P.M. LHO is confronted in the lunchroom of the Texas School Book Depository Building, where he works, by Patrolman Marrion Baker. The superintendent of the building, Roy Truly, vouches for LHO, and he is released.

Texas School Book Depository outside view

View from Texas Book Depository Window, shooter's view

12:33 P.M. LHO leaves the school book depository by the front door.

Texas School Book Depository

Sniper's nest in Texas School Book Depository

12:40 P.M. LHO boards a bus to make his escape.

The bus LHO rode during his escape

12:44 P.M. LHO leaves the bus when it becomes bogged down in traffic.

12:48 P.M. LHO hails a cab and asks to be taken to 500 North Beckley.

12:54 P.M. LHO exits the cab in the 700 block of North Beckley.

01:00 P.M. LHO arrives on foot at his rooming house, where he retrieves his pistol.

01:03 P.M. LHO leaves the rooming house.

01:15 P.M. LHO is stopped and questioned by Dallas police officer J. D. Tippit.

Officer J. D. Tippit

Tippit crime scene

01:16 P.M. LHO shoots Officer J. D. Tippit and continues fleeing.

01:22 P.M. Police broadcast a description of the suspect in the Tippit murder.

01:40 P.M. LHO enters the Texas Theatre.

01:48 P.M. Police enter the theater.

Texas Theatre interior

01:50 P.M. After a struggle with police in the Texas Theatre, LHO is captured.

Arresting LHO at the Texas Theatre

While Oswald is fleeing, doctors are frantically trying to save the life of President Kennedy.

- *At 12:50 P.M., while Oswald was walking to his room, doctors stop working on JFK. They step aside to allow the Reverend Oscar Huber to perform the last rites of the Catholic Church.*

- *During the next four minutes, doctors officially declare JFK dead at Parkland Hospital. Shortly after 1:00 P.M., Attorney General Robert Kennedy receives a phone call at his home in Virginia informing him that the wounds his brother suffered proved fatal.*

At 1:00 P.M., as Oswald returns to his boarding house, JFK is pronounced dead. LBJ learns that JFK is dead at the same time that Oswald is confronted by Officer Tippit.

JFK autopsy report

01:58 P.M. LHO arrives at Dallas police headquarters.

02:30 P.M. LHO is first questioned by Dallas police.
(Roughly 2:30—at 2:25 Fritz enters the police interrogation room.)

PARALLEL MOMENTS

According to the official Secret Service log, the presidential party arrived at Love Field airport in Dallas at 2:14 P.M., just as the formal interrogation of Lee Harvey Oswald was about to begin.

At 2:40 P.M., as Oswald is being questioned for the first time, LBJ takes the oath of office. A few minutes later, the plane lifts off for the trip back to Washington, D.C.

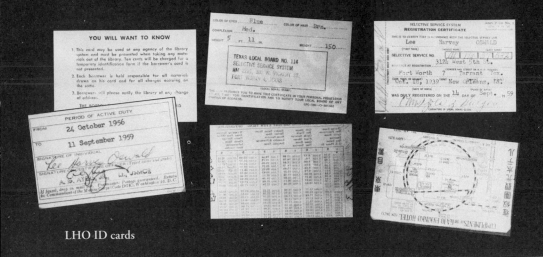

LHO ID cards

03:15 P.M. FBI agent James P. Hosty Jr. enters the interrogation room.

04:00 P.M. Officers arrive at Oswald's North Beckley rooming house.

04:30 P.M. LHO is taken to the basement for the first lineup.

04:35 P.M. LHO enters the lineup under the number two.

PARALLEL MOMENTS

At 5:58 P.M., *Air Force One* touches down at Andrews Air Force Base outside Washington. JFK's body comes off the plane, followed by Jacqueline Kennedy. Then LBJ proceeds to deliver a brief speech as the body of JFK is prepared to be moved from the aircraft.

"This is a sad time for all people. We have suffered a loss that cannot be weighed. For me, is a deep personal tragedy. I know the world shares the sorrow that Mrs. Kennedy and her family bear. I will do my best. That is all I can do. I ask for your help—and God's." —LBJ

PARALLEL MOMENTS

While police are interrogating Oswald, doctors at Bethesda Naval Hospital begin their autopsy of JFK's body. It is difficult to determine the trajectory of the bullet. Additionally, Jackie Kennedy has decided to have the funeral preparation rites modeled after President Lincoln's service.

06:20 P.M. LHO is taken for the second lineup.

06:35 P.M. LHO is returned upstairs for questioning.

07:10 P.M. LHO is formally arraigned for the murder of Tippit.

07:28 P.M. LHO is led through the crush of reporters at the Dallas police station.

07:40 P.M. LHO is taken for the third lineup.

07:55 P.M. LHO announces that he is "a patsy."

11:26 P.M. Dallas police file charges against LHO for the assassination of President John F. Kennedy.

LHO poses for a mug shot

At this time JFK's body is continuing to be examined. The doctors have an exceptionally difficult time reconstructing the skull so it will be fit for public viewing.

SATURDAY, NOVEMBER 23

12:05 A.M. (approx.): LHO appears before the media in the basement.

12:07 A.M. Jack Ruby stands a few feet from LHO.

12:10 A.M. LHO is led out in front of another press conference. He is informed by a reporter that he has been charged with the murder of JFK.

12:20 A.M. LHO is returned to his cell.

12:35 A.M. LHO poses for a mug shot.

01:30 A.M. LHO is formally arraigned for the murder of JFK.

08:00 A.M. LHO is served breakfast.

10:25 A.M. Another day of questioning begins.

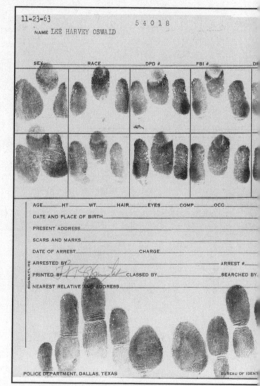

LHO fingerprints

11:27 A.M. LHO tells reporters he wants to be represented by a lawyer named John Abt from the American Civil Liberties Union.

11:35 A.M. LHO is returned to his cell.

Jack Ruby in the Dallas Police Department hallway

PARALLEL MOMENTS

At 3:30 A.M., doctors at Bethesda Naval Hospital finish their painstaking work on the president's head wound. Kennedy's valet, George Thomas, brings clothes. "He had four summer suits and four winter suits, and two good pairs of brown shoes and two good black pairs." They agree on the selection of a blue-gray suit and a blue tie. They place a white handkerchief in his pocket.

At 3:56 A.M., the president's coffin is loaded into a hearse for the thirty-five-minute drive back to the White House. The following morning, while Oswald is being interrogated, Mrs. Kennedy gathers items that JFK cherished and places them lovingly into his coffin. Jackie kisses her husband, cuts off two locks of his hair, and places them in small ceramic frames. She keeps one lock for herself and gives the other to Bobby.

- Workers spend most of the night and the early morning preparing the East Room for the viewing.

- Arthur Schlesinger Jr. described the scene as Kennedy returned to the White House for the last time. "The casket was carried into the East Room and deposited on a stand. It was wrapped in a flag. Jackie followed, accompanied by Bobby. . . . a priest said a few words. Then Bobby whispered to Jackie. Then she walked away. The rest of us followed."

- Soon after the president's body arrives back at the White House, Jackie goes to her room, but Bobby Kennedy returns and asks presidential aide Arthur Schlesinger to view the body and make a recommendation about whether to have an open casket. He records his thoughts in his journal later that day. "And so I went in, with the candles fitfully burning, three priests on their knees praying in the background, and took a last look at my beloved president, my beloved friend," he wrote. "For a moment, I was shattered. But it was not a good job, probably it could not have been with half his head blasted away. It was too waxen, too made up. It did not really look like him." Schlesinger reports back to Bobby who makes the decision to have a closed coffin.

- At 10:00 A.M., about seventy-five Kennedy family members and close friends attend what many believe is the first Catholic mass ever held in the White House.

- "The whole family was like a bunch of shipwreck survivors," said JFK friend Lem Billings. "I don't think they could have made it at all without Bobby. He seemed to be everywhere. He always had an arm around a friend or family member and was telling them it was okay, that it was time to move ahead."

- At noon, Mrs. Kennedy makes arrangements for the state funeral scheduled for Monday. Robert McNamara goes to Arlington National Cemetery and finds the spot where he believes JFK would want to be buried. LBJ works the phones, consolidating power.

12:35 P.M. LHO is taken to Fritz's office for questioning.

01:10 P.M. Marina Oswald, LHO's wife, and his mother, Marguerite Oswald, visit LHO.

01:40 P.M. LHO tries unsuccessfully to contact attorney John Abt.

02:00 P.M. LBJ calls Mrs. Tippit.

02:15 P.M. LHO appears in a fourth lineup.

02:45 P.M. Fingernail scrapings and hair samples are obtained from LHO with his permission.

03:37 P.M. LHO's brother Robert visits LHO.

04:00–4:30 P.M.
LHO phones family friend Ruth Paine and asks her to try to obtain John Abt as his attorney.

05:45 P.M. LHO is visited by the president of the Dallas Bar Association, H. Louis Nichols.

06:27 P.M. LHO is taken again for questioning.

07:15 P.M. LHO is returned to his cell.

08:00 P.M. Jack Ruby is inconsolable, grieving over the death of JFK.

SUNDAY, NOVEMBER 24

09:30 A.M. LHO is signed out of jail in anticipation of a transfer to the county facility.

11:15 A.M. The transfer party leaves Fritz's office after a final round of questions.

11:20 A.M Jack Ruby enters the underground garage.

11:21 A.M LHO is shot by Jack Ruby in the basement of the Dallas city jail.

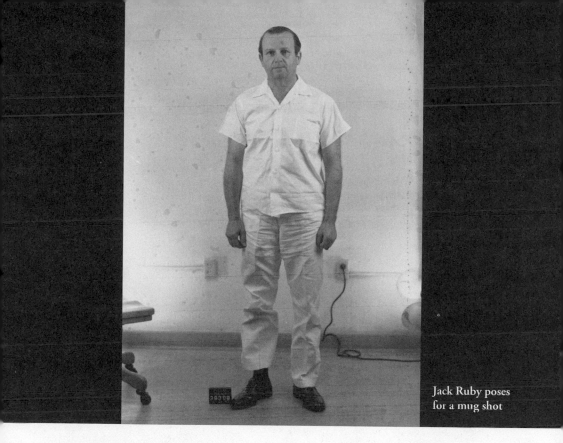

Jack Ruby poses
for a mug shot

11:23 A.M. LHO is given a last chance to confess to killing JFK.
He refuses.

11:23 A.M. A medical student who happens to be on the scene tries
to stabilize LHO.

11:26 A.M. An ambulance arrives.

PARALLEL MOMENTS

At the time Jack Ruby shoots Lee Harvey Oswald, Mrs. Kennedy and Robert F. Kennedy are kneeling before the open coffin, saying their final goodbye to the slain president.

Outside, a crowd of three hundred thousand people stand under the bright sun lining the two-mile route from the White House to the Capitol. Those who have transistor radios spread the word of the shooting in Dallas of Lee Harvey Oswald.

11:35 A.M. A Parkland Hospital doctor refuses to treat LHO in same room as JFK had been treated just two days before.

11:40 A.M. The same team of doctors that treated JFK is now trying to save his assassin.

01:07 P.M. LHO is pronounced dead at the Parkland Hospital— 48 hours and seven minutes after JFK.

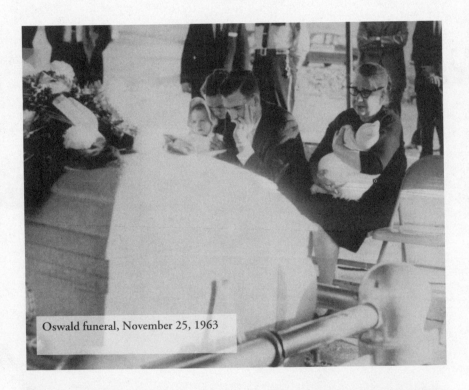

Oswald funeral, November 25, 1963

PARALLEL MOMENTS

In Washington, mourners stand in lines that stretch for forty blocks to pay their respects to JFK as word continues to spread that Oswald has been shot.

ENDNOTES

The *President's Commission on the Assassination of President John F. Kennedy* (Washington, D.C.: United States Government Printing Office, 1964), generally called the *Warren Commission Report*, was supported by 26 volumes (labeled 1 H–24 H) of testimony (volumes H 1–H 15) and exhibits (volumes H 16–H 26), with volumes H19–H21 comprised of deposition exhibits. Each volume carries the name *Investigation of the Assassination of President John F. Kennedy: Hearings before the President's Commission on the Assassination of President John F. Kennedy*. Appendix 18 of the *Warren Commission Report* provides footnotes to this, and other material, cited in the *Report*. In doing so, the *Warren Commission Report* uses the following citation format for **testimony:** number of volume, "H" for "*Hearings before the President's Commission on the Assassination of President Kennedy,*" page number in the volume, and the name of the witness in parentheses, e.g., 4 H 130 (Forrest V. Sorrels). **Commission Exhibits** found in volumes H 16–H 18 and H 22–H 26 use the symbol of the capital letters "CE" and the number of the exhibit, e.g., CE 1024. **Deposition Exhibits** found in volumes H 19–H 21 carry the format, name of witness, "DE" for deposition exhibit, and the number or letter of the exhibit, e.g., Forrest V. Sorrels DE 1. The footnotes that follow use the same formatting scheme used in the *Warren Commission Report* with the exception that both Commission Exhibits and Deposition Exhibits include a volume number (e.g., 16 H) and, if relevant, page number(s).

PREFACE

[1] John, who was a close friend, shared this story with the author shortly after John's return from Cuba.

CHAPTER 1

"Want to See a Secret Service Agent?"

[1] Priscilla McMillan, *Marina and Lee* (New York: Bantam, 1978), 564.

[2] Vincent Bugliosi, *Reclaiming History: The Assassination of President John F. Kennedy,* (New York: W.W. Norton, 2007), 3–5; McMillan, *Marina and Lee*, 564.

[3] Bugliosi, *Reclaiming History*, 6; McMillan, *Marina and Lee*, 566–67.

[4] McMillan, *Marina and Lee*, 566.

[5] Copy of memorandum by Dave Powers, (ND), William Manchester Papers, Wesleyan University Special Collections and Archives (WM–WU), Middletown, CT.

[6] Bugliosi, *Reclaiming History*, 33; Jack Valenti, "One Day's Passage of Power," *Washington Post*, November 21, 1963.

[7] Michael L. Kurtz, *The JFK Assassination Debates: Lone Gunman versus Conspiracy* (Lawrence: University of Kansas, 2006), 3–4.

[8] James Leavelle, Oral History Collection, Sixth Floor Museum at Dealey Plaza Sixth Floor, (June 6, 2002), 22.

[9] Gerald Posner, *Case Closed: Lee Harvey Oswald and the Assassination of JFK* (New York: Anchor Books, 1993), 113–15, According to conspiracy author Robert J. Groden, the CIA, not Marina, sent Oswald to New Orleans to ingratiate himself with pro-Castro groups in order to penetrate Cuban intelligence and perhaps travel to Havana where he could assassinate Castro. The confrontation with anti-Castro groups was — like everything else in Oswald's life — orchestrated by the CIA in order "to build up Oswald's image, or 'legend,' as an antisocial and violent loner and a supporter of Fidel Castro." Robert J. Groden, *The Search for Lee Harvey Oswald* (New York: Penguin, 1995), 88–89.

[10] Some conspiracy advocates maintain that Oswald never went to Mexico City.

Instead, the "intelligence community" sent an imposter as part of an elaborate plot to frame Oswald. "There is no tangible proof that Lee went to Mexico City," wrote conspiracy author Robert J. Groden. "There is far more evidence that one or more imposters and not the genuine Lee Oswald actually went to Mexico." See: Groden, *The Search for Lee Harvey Oswald*, 80.

[11] James P. Hosty Jr., *Assignment: Oswald* (New York: Arcade Publishing, 2011), 213–14.

[12] Norman Mailer, *Oswald's Tale: An American Mystery* (New York: Random House, 1995), 786.

CHAPTER 2

"Attention All Squads . . . Attention All Squads"

[1] Mimi Swartz, "The Witness," *Texas Monthly*, November 2003, 114.

[2] CE 1024 18 H 755; Emory Roberts interview, December 4, 1964 (WM–WU).

[3] Swartz, "The Witness," 114; White notes, December 19, 1963 (WM–WU).

[4] Evan Thomas, "The Real Cover-Up," *Newsweek*, November 22, 1963, 66; George Ball Interview, April 10, 1964 (WM–WU).

[5] Judy Whitson Bonner, *Investigation of a Homicide: The Murder of John F. Kennedy*, (New York: Droke House, 1969), 56.

[6] Jim Bishop, *The Day Kennedy Was Shot* (New York: Gramercy, 1984), 183; Bonner, *Investigation of a Homicide*, 56.

[7] William Manchester, *The Death of a President: November 1963* (New York: Harper, 1967), 279.

[8] Ibid.

[9] Ibid., 280.

[10] "Johnson Takes Oath," *Los Angeles Times*, November 23, 1963, 1; Bugliosi, *Reclaiming History*, 58; Gerald Posner, *Case Closed: Lee Harvey Oswald and the Assassination of JFK* (New York: Anchor Books, 1993), 287.

[11] Bishop, *Day Kennedy Was Shot*, 210–11.

[12] CE 705 17 H ; 4 H 184 (Jesse Edward Curry).

[13] Bonner, *Investigation of a Homicide,* 68–69.

[14] Manchester, *Death of a President,* 280–81.

[15] Bishop, *Day Kennedy Was Shot,* 218.

[16] Ibid., 223–24.

[17] Ibid., 234–35.

[18] Manchester, *Death of a President,* 281

[19] See: http://www.maryferrell.org/mffweb/archive/viewer/showDoc.do?docId=800&relPageId=539. Thanks to Jean Davidson for sharing this information with me.

[20] Author interview with Jean Davidson, March 4, 2013.

[21] Author interview with Jean Davidson, March 4, 2013; author interview with John McAdams, February 27, 2013.

[22] Author interview with Gerald Posner, October 19, 2012; author interview with Max Holland, February 27, 2013.

[23] Posner, interview, October 19, 2012.

[24] Posner, *Case Closed,* 272.

CHAPTER 3

"Somebody Shot a Police Officer"

[1] Dale K. Myers, *With Malice: Lee Harvey Oswald and the Murder of Officer J.D. Tippit,* (Milford, Michigan: Oak Cliff Press, 1998),55–56.

[2] Bishop, *Day Kennedy Was Shot,* 256–57.

[3] Manchester, *Death of a President,* 282; Bishop, *Day Kennedy Was Shot,* 257.

[4] Myers, *With Malice,* 84–93.

[5] 4 H 184 (Jesse Edward Curry).

[6] Posner, *Case Closed,* 369–70.

[7] Ibid., 371.

[8] Ibid., 371.

[9] Jean Daniel, "When Castro Heard the News," *New Republic* (December 7, 1963), 7–9.

CHAPTER 4

"Well, It Is All Over Now"

[1] Bonner, *Investigation of a Homicide*, 105–6; Paul Bentley, Oral History Collection, Sixth Floor Museum at Dealey Plaza Sixth Floor, (February 16, 1994), 8.

[2] "Officer Recalls Oswald Capture," *Dallas Morning News*, November 24, 1963, 13.

[3] Bishop, *Day Kennedy Was Shot*, 276–77.

[4] Larry A. Sneed, *No More Silence: An Oral History of the Assassination of President Kennedy*, (Denton: University of North Texas, 2002), 297–98.

[5] 7 H 57–58 (Gerald Lynn Hill); 7 H 40–41(C. T. Walker); Dallas Police Tapes, C1:1:52–53.

[6] Bonner, *Investigation of a Homicide*, 109–10.

[7] Bentley, Oral History, Sixth Floor Museum, 10. While Bentley claims that he spoke with the police dispatcher there are no tapes to confirm these conversations took place.

[8] Manchester, *Death of a President*, 276.

[9] Price Memo, November 27, 1963 (WM–WU); Bishop, *Day Kennedy Was Shot*, 283.

[10] Bishop, *Day Kennedy Was Shot*, 284; Bugliosi, *Reclaiming History*, 92.

[11] Bishop, *Day Kennedy Was Shot*, 284–85.

[12] Bentley, Oral History Collection, Sixth Floor Museum at Dealey Plaza Sixth Floor, (February 16, 1994), 16.

[13] Bonner, *Investigation of a Homicide*, 119–20.

[14] Sneed, *No More Silence*, 298; Bishop, *Day Kennedy Was Shot*, 331; Bonner, *Investigation of a Homicide*, 120.

[15] Sneed, Ibid., 389.

CHAPTER 5

". . . There He Sits"

[1] Bugliosi, *Reclaiming History*, 114.

[2] Sneed, *No More Silence*, 269–72.

³ Ibid., 121–23.

⁴ Bugliosi, *Reclaiming History*, 114–15.

⁵ Sneed, *No More Silence*, 298–99.

⁶ Since the Dallas police did not use a tape recorder, no written record of the interrogation exists. In his book, *Reclaiming History*, the author Bugliosi offers what appears to be a detailed, transcript-like, account of the conversations between Oswald and Fritz. In reality, Bugliosi has recreated the interrogations. He turned general characterizations about topics into actual dialogue. His recreations are fair-minded, and based on a meticulous knowledge of the material. I was uncomfortable, however, putting words in Oswald's mouth. I have only attributed to Oswald words that others in the room have claimed were direct quotes. There were two exceptions. I relied on the accounts of two journalists, Jim Bishop (*The Day Kennedy Was Shot*) and Judy Whitson Bonner (*Investigation of a Homicide*). Since they wrote their books soon after the assassination, and had access to many of the major players, I am assuming that they used standard journalistic practices and only used quotes directly attributable to Oswald.

⁷ Bonner, *Investigation of a Homicide*, 14–15.

⁸ Sneed, *No More Silence*, 269–72; Bonner, *Investigation of a Homicide*, 122–23.

⁹ 4 H 210–13 (John Will Fritz).

¹⁰ Ibid., 213.

CHAPTER 6

"Squirming Like a Snared Rat"

¹ McMillan, *Marina and Lee* , 532–33

² Hosty, *Assignment: Oswald*, 9–11.

³ Ibid., 16.

⁴ Ibid., 18–19.

⁵ Ibid., 19.

⁶ Ibid., 20; Elmer Boyd, Oral History Collection, Sixth Floor Museum at Dealey Plaza, (February 22, 2007), 8.

[7] Hosty, *Assignment Oswald*, 22–25. The dialogue that follows has been adapted from Hosty's account of the interrogation.

CHAPTER 7

Don't Care to Answer Any More Questions"

[1] George Ball, *The Past as Another Pattern: Memoirs* (New York: Norton, 1983), 311.

[2] Ibid., 312.

[3] General Chester Clifton interview, April 21, 1964 (WM–WU).

[4] Forrest V. Sorrels interview, September 24, 1964, Box 44 (WM–WU).

[5] 7 H 353 (Forrest V. Sorrels) ; Bishop, *Day Kennedy Was Shot*, 316.

[6] Hosty, *Assignment: Oswald*, 28; 7 H 353 (Sorrels).

[7] 7 H 353 (Sorrels).

[8] Sorrels, Box 44 (WM–WU).

[9] 7 H 353 (Sorrels), 353–54.

[10] Bonner, *Investigation of a Homicide,* 142–46.

[11] Evan Thomas, *Robert Kennedy: A Life* (New York: Simon and Schuster, 2002), 277.

[12] Author interview with Brian Latell, February 26, 2013.

CHAPTER 8:

"Did You Kill the President?"

[1] Stephen Fagin, "November 1963: Dallas Police vs. the World Press," *Legacies* (Fall 2006), 37–38.

[2] James Leavelle, Oral History Collection, Sixth Floor Museum at Dealey Plaza Sixth Floor, (June 6, 2002), 24; Fagin, "November 1963," 38.

[3] Fagin, "November 1963," 40.

⁴ Ibid., 44.

⁵ 7 H 268 (James R. Leavelle).

⁶ Bugliosi, *Reclaiming History*, 132.

⁷ 7 H 126, 136 (Elmer L. Boyd).; 7 H 173 (Richard M. Sims); Bugliosi, *Reclaiming History*, 132–33; Elmer Boyd, Oral History Collection, Sixth Floor Museum at Dealey Plaza, (February 22, 2007), 18.

⁸ 7 H 166–168 (Sims); James R. Leavelle DE A 20 H 499–503.

⁹ Bishop, *Day Kennedy Was Shot*, 183; Bonner, *Investigation of a Homicide,*, 278–79.

¹⁰ Ibid., 358.

¹¹ Bugliosi, *Reclaiming History*, 128–29; Bishop, 359–60.

¹² Bishop, *Day Kennedy Was Shot*, 260–61; Bonner, *Investigation of a Homicide*, 138.

CHAPTER 9

"The Number-Two Man"

¹ DE A 20 H 499–503. A. (James R. Leavelle)

² 7 H 171–72 (Richard M. Sims); Bishop, *Day Kennedy Was Shot*, 459.

³ 7 H 151–52 (C. N. Dhority); Bishop, *Day Kennedy Was Shot*, 458.

⁴ 4 H 215, 225 (John Will Fritz).

⁵ Gary Wills and Ovid Demaris, *Jack Ruby* (New York: Da Capo Press, 1994), 70.

⁶ Bugliosi, *Reclaiming History*, 152–53; Bishop, *Day Kennedy Was Shot*, 470; "Oswald Arrogance Irks Prosecutor," *Dallas Morning News*, November 24, 1963, 3.

⁷ "Oswald Arrogance Irks Prosecutor," *Dallas Morning News*, 3.

⁸ Bishop, *Day Kennedy Was Shot*, 492.

⁹ Bugliosi, *Reclaiming History*, 643–44.

¹⁰ Marguerite Oswald, September 18, 1964, Box 45 (WM–WU).

¹¹ Bishop, *Day Kennedy Was Shot*, 494–495.

¹² Marguerite Oswald, September 18, 1964, Box 45 (WM–WU).

[13] Bugliosi, *Reclaiming History*, 156.

[14] 7 H 172 (Sims); Bugliosi, *Reclaiming History*, 159–60.

[15] Arthur Schlesinger Jr. Journal (WM–WU).

CHAPTER 10

"I Know the Tactics of the FBI"

[1] 4 H 356 (Winston G. Lawson).

[2] 7 H 30 (Elmer L. Boyd); Bugliosi, *Reclaiming History*, 161.

[3] Bugliosi, *Reclaiming History*, 163.

[4] Bugliosi, *Reclaiming History*, 164; Bishop, *Day Kennedy Was Shot*, 516.

[5] 7 H 173, 180 (Richard M. Sims); Bugliosi, *Reclaiming History*, 165; Bishop, *Day Kennedy Was Shot*, 516–17.

[6] Bugliosi, *Reclaiming History*, 165–66.

[7] Ibid., 166.

[8] Bonner, *Investigation of a Homicide*, 151.

[9] Ibid., 153–54.

[10] Ibid., 154; Bugliosi, *Reclaiming History*, 167.

[11] Wills and Demaris, *Jack Ruby*.

[12] Horace Busby, et al., *The Thirty-First of March: An Intimate Portrait of Lyndon Johnson's Final Days in Office* (New York: Farrar, Straus and Giroux, 2006), 153.

CHAPTER 11

"He Is Really a Good Boy"

[1] Bugliosi, *Reclaiming History*, 182.

[2] Ibid., 182–83.

[3] Sneed, *No More Silence*, 278.

[4] Bugliosi, *Reclaiming History*, 176.

⁵ Ike Pappas, Oral History, Sixth Floor Museum, (March 1, 1993), 7–8.

⁶ Manchester, *Death of a President*, 415–16.

⁷ Theodore White Notes, December 19, 1963 (WM–WU).

CHAPTER 12

"You Have Been Charged"

¹ 4 H 166 (Jesse Edward Curry).

² Posner, *Case Closed*, 378.

³ Sneed, *No More Silence*, 257.

⁴ Ibid., 138.

⁵ Bugliosi, *Reclaiming History*, 191; Kurtz, *JFK Assassination Debates*, 18.

⁶ Bishop, *Day Kennedy Was Shot*, 384–85.

⁷ Ibid., 385.

⁸ Ibid., 386.

⁹ Ibid., 386–87.

¹⁰ 7 H 128 (Elmer L. Boyd); 4 H 154 Jesse Edward Curry).

¹¹ Bugliosi, *Reclaiming History*, 193–94; 15H 508 (David L. Johnston); 4H 156 (Jesse Edward Curry).

¹² "Chronology of NBC Coverage of the Assassination" (WM–WU).

¹³ Forrest Sorrels interview, September 24, 1964 (WM–WU).

¹⁴ Ike Pappas, Oral History Collection, Sixth Floor Museum at Dealey Plaza Sixth Floor, (March 1, 1993), 8.

¹⁵ Bugliosi, *Reclaiming History*, 200–201; Posner, *Case Closed*, 380.

¹⁶ Posner, *Case Closed*, 380–82; DE 5402 21 H 433–36 (George Senator).

¹⁷ Dave Powers, April 8, 1964 (WM–WU).

¹⁸ Schlesinger Journal, November 22, 1963, 5:15 a.m. (WM–WU).

CHAPTER 13

"My Wife and I Like the President's Family"

[1] Bugliosi, *Reclaiming History*, 204; Bonner, *Investigation of a Homicide*, 173.

[2] Sally Bedell Smith, *Grace and Power: The Private World of the Kennedy White House* (New York: Random House, 2004), 446–46.

[3] Johnson used an IBM machine designed for taking dictation to record his phone conversations. Oddly enough, the conversation with Hoover was taped, and secretaries prepared a transcript and then destroyed the tape. This was the only recording that was destroyed. (Max Holland, *The Kennedy Assassination Tapes: The White House Conversations of Lyndon B. Johnson Regarding the Assassination, the Warren Commission, and the Aftermath* (New York: Knopf, 2004), 69–71.

[4] Holland, *Kennedy Assassination Tapes*, 72–73.

[5] Bugliosi, *Reclaiming History*, 213.

[6] 7 H 314–315 (James W. Bookhout).

[7] Sorrels, Box 44 (WM–WU).

[8] Bugliosi, *Reclaiming History*, 213–14.

[9] Ibid., 214.

[10] CE 198824 H 19.

[11] Bugliosi, *Reclaiming History*, 216; CE 1988 24 H 19; DE A 20 H 440 (Thomas J. Kelley).

[12] CE 198824 H 19; Bugliosi, *Reclaiming History*, 216.

[13] CE 1988 24 H 19.

[14] 7 H 314 (Bookhout); 7 H 354–355 (Sorrels).

[15] Bugliosi, *Reclaiming History*, 216–17; Bishop, *Day Kennedy Was Shot*, 302.

[16] Bishop, *Day Kennedy Was Shot*, 302; Bugliosi, *Reclaiming History*, 217.

[17] Bishop, *Day Kennedy Was Shot*, 302–3; Bugliosi, *Reclaiming History*, 218; Kelly DE A 20 H 441 (Kelley). Conspiracy theorists who believed that Oswald was in fact a double agent have dismissed the two days of interrogation. The historian David Kaiser simply claimed that Oswald stayed "in character as a left-wing activist" throughout the sessions. See: David Kaiser, *The Road to Dallas: The Assassination of John F. Kennedy* (Cambridge: Harvard University Press, 2008).

¹⁸ 7 H 314–15 (Bookhout).

¹⁹ Bugliosi, *Reclaiming History,* 218; 7 H 314–15 (Bookhout).

²⁰ Bugliosi, *Reclaiming History,* 219.

²¹ Nicholas Katzenbach interview, June 5, 1964 (WM–WU).

²² John McCone, "Memorandum for the Record," November 25, 1963, Lyndon B. Johnson Presidential Library (LBJL), Meeting Notes File, Box 1, p 1.

²³ Ibid.; Holland, *Kennedy Assassination Tapes,* 69.

CHAPTER 14

"Brother, You Won't Find Anything There"

¹ McMillan, *Marina and Lee,* 585.

² Ibid., 435.

³ Ibid., 588.

⁴ Ibid., 588; Bugliosi, *Reclaiming History,* 224

⁵ Bugliosi, *Reclaiming History,* 224; 1H 149 (Marguerite Oswald); Marguerite Oswald interview, September 18, 1964, Box 45 (WM–WU).

⁶ Bugliosi, *Reclaiming History,* 224; 1H 150 (Marguerite Oswald); McMillan, *Marina and Lee,* 588.

⁷ McMillan, *Marina and Lee,* 588–89. Marina would later change her position and insist that her husband was innocent. She could not, however, take back the damaging evidence that she had provided against him.

⁸ Bishop, *Day Kennedy Was Shot,* 398–99.

⁹ DE A 20 H (Leavelle).

¹⁰ Bugliosi, *Reclaiming History,* 227.

¹¹ Ibid.

¹² Ibid.

¹³ "NBC Chronology," Box 44 (WM–WU).

¹⁴ Gary Mack, "Police Chief Jesse Curry: a Kennedy Assassination Victim?" *Legacies* (Fall 2006), 24.

¹⁵ Posner, *Case Closed,* 385.

[16] Robert Oswald, *Lee: A Portrait of Lee Harvey Oswald by His Brother* (New York: Coward–McCann, 1967), 17.

[17] Ibid., 142–43; Robert Oswald interview, November 5, 1964, Box 44 (WM–WU).

[18] This dialogue is adapted from Oswald, *Lee,* 142–46.

[19] Bugliosi, *Reclaiming History,* 231.

[20] Ibid., 233.

[21] Ibid., 234–35.

[22] 7 H316 (Bookout); 7 H 231(Guy F. Rose); 4 H 266 (Fritz).

[23] 7 H 315–17 (Bookhout).

[24] 4H 226 (Fritz).

[25] Bugliosi, *Reclaiming History,* 238.

[26] Ibid., 239.

[27] "Testimony and Documents of the Presidential Commission," Box 45 (WM–WU).

[28] Bonner, *Investigation of a Homicide,* 177.

[29] Marguerite later told William Manchester a similar story. She recognized Ruby's picture when it appeared on Monday in the *Star-Telegram.* She told a Secret Service agent, "this is the man whose picture the FBI showed me." The agent responded, "that's the man who killed your son." The most likely explanation is that Marguerite was confused about the dates. She was probably shown the mug shot of Ruby on Sunday night, after her son was shot, and then saw Ruby's picture in the paper the following morning. Marguerite Oswald interview, September 18, 1964, Box 45 (WM–WU). Her interview with the Secret Service can be found at: http://www.history-matters.com/archive/jfk/wc/wcvols/wh16/html/WH_Vol16_0373a.htm.

CHAPTER 15

"I Don't Know What You Are Talking About"

[1] 7 H 269 (Leavelle).

[2] Sneed, *No More Silence,* 359–60.

³ 7 H 297 (Harry D. Holmes).

⁴ Bugliosi, *Reclaiming History*, 252–53; 7 H 267–68 (Leavelle).

⁵ DE A 20 H 444 (Kelley).

⁶ 7 H 297–98 (Holmes).

⁷ Ibid.

⁸ Ibid.

⁹ James R. Leavelle, Oral History Collection, Sixth Floor Museum at Dealey Plaza Sixth Floor, (June 10, 2002), 18.

¹⁰ 7 H 301–2 (Holmes).

¹¹ Leavelle, Oral History, Sixth Floor Museum, 18.

¹² 7 H 299 (Holmes).

¹³ Ibid., 302.

¹⁴ CE 2064 24 H 491.

¹⁵ 7 H 303 (Holmes).

¹⁶ Ibid., 304.

¹⁷ Ibid., 305.

¹⁸ Ibid., 297; 7 H 354–55 (Sorrels).

¹⁹ 7 H 299 (Holmes).

²⁰ Posner, *Case Closed*, 391.

²¹ 14 H 164 (Senator); Wills and Demaris, *Jack Ruby*, 50–54.

²² Posner, *Case Closed*, 391.

CHAPTER 16

"... You're Just Being Melodramatic"

¹ 12 H 4 (Charles Batchelor); James R. Leavelle, Oral History, Sixth Floor Museum at Dealey Plaza, (June 10, 2002), 25. Fritz was convinced that it was Jack Ruby who made the call during the night threatening Oswald. "I have always felt that that was Ruby who made that call, I may be wrong, but he was out late that night and I have always felt he might have made that call, if two or three of those officers had started out with him they may have had the same trouble they had the next morning."

² Leavelle, Oral History, Sixth Floor Museum, 25.

³ Ibid., 25.

⁴ Forrest Sorrels interview, September 24, 1964 (WM–WU).

⁵ Bugliosi, *Reclaiming History*, 265.

⁶ 13 H 5 (L.C. Graves); 7 H 357 (Sorrels).

⁷ Bonner, *Investigation of a Homicide,*,181.

⁸ Wills and Demaris, *Jack Ruby*, 56.

⁹ Gary Mack, "Police Chief Jesse Curry: A Kennedy Assassination Victim?" *Legacies* (Fall 2006), 27.

¹⁰ Leavelle, Oral History, Sixth Floor Museum, 26.

¹¹ Ibid., 30.

CHAPTER 17

"You Killed My President, You Rat Son of a Bitch"

¹ Ike Pappas, Oral History, Sixth Floor Museum (March 1, 1993), 9–10.

² Sneed, *No More Silence*, 377–78.

³ Wills and Demaris *Jack Ruby*, 74.

⁴ 13 H 5 (Graves).

⁵ Stephen Fagin, "November 1963: Dallas Police vs. the World Press," *Legacies* (Fall 2006), 36.

⁶ At his trial, a number of witnesses offered conflicting testimony about exactly what words Ruby used when he shot Oswald. Most accounts, however, claim he called him a "rat" and "a son of a bitch," although the ordering of the words vary. Whatever Ruby said was not picked up by the microphones stationed in the room.

⁷ DE 5089 20 H 506–7 (Leavelle).

⁸ 13 H 8 (Graves); Graves, Oral History, Sixth Floor Museum (March 2, 1994), 18–19; 13 H 29 (L. D. Montgomery).

⁹ Sneed, *No More Silence,* 396–97.

¹⁰ "Millions of Viewers See Oswald Killing on 2 TV Networks," *New York Times*, November 25, 1963.

CHAPTER 18

"I Hope I Killed the Son of a Bitch"

[1] Manchester, *Death of a President*, 515–17.

[2] DE 5123 19 H 163–66 (Dr. Fred A. Bieberdorf); Forrest Sorrels interview, September 24, 1964, (WM–WU).

[3] 13 H 30, 33 (Montgomery); Wills and Demaris, *Jack Ruby*, 71.

[4] DE 5123 19 H 163–166 (Bieberdorf).

[5] Ibid.

[6] Ibid.

[7] Sneed, *No More Silence*, 398.

[8] "NBC Chronology" (WM–WU).

[9] 3 H 384–87 (Malcolm Perry).

[10] Posner, *Case Closed*, 396; 13 H 67–68 (Sorrels).

[11] Posner, *Case Closed,* 397.

EPILOGUE

[1] Oswald Is Buried in Texas in a Wooden Coffin," *New York Times*, November 26, 1963.

[2] "Oswald, Accused Assassin, Buried; 4 of Family Attend," *Los Angeles Times*, November 26, 1963.

[3] 3 H 312 (Bookout).

[4] 3 H 173, 180 (Sims).

[5] 7 H 135 (Boyd); Elmer Boyd, Oral History Collection, Sixth Floor Museum (February 22, 2007), 9.

[6] 7 H 269 (Leavelle).

[7] "New Yorkers Are Horrified by Slaying of Oswald," *New York Times*, November 25, 1963; "Oswald Death Unbelievable? *Dallas Morning News*, November 25, 1963, 2; "Oh, My God — He's Dead," *Dallas Morning News*, November 25, 1963, 7.

[8] Arthur Schlesinger Jr. Journal (WM–WU).

[9] "Other Countries Hear Quickly about Shooting," *Washington Post*, November 25, 1963.

[10] Manchester, *Death of a President*, 525.

[11] Ibid., 525–27.

[12] Ibid., 518, 525.

[13] Ibid., 528.

[14] Vincent Bugliosi has effectively demolished all of these theories in his masterful account of the assassination and the investigation, *Reclaiming History*. Also valuable is the little-known book by Larry M. Sturdivan, *The JFK Myths: A Scientific Investigation of the Kennedy Assassination*, (St. Paul, MN: Paragon House, 2005).

[15] Kaiser, *Road to Dallas*, introduction.

[16] Kurtz, *JFK Assassination Debates*, 164.

[17] Groden, *Search for Lee Harvey Oswald*, 26. For a scathing, but justified, analysis of David Kaiser's book see: John McAdams, "Road to Nowhere," *Washington Decoded*, March 11, 2008.

[18] Brian Latell, *Castro's Secrets: The CIA and Cuba's Intelligence Machine* (New York: Palgrave MacMillan), 143–44; Kaiser, *Road to Dallas*.

[19] Brian Latell, *Castro's Secrets*, 140–41.

[20] Bugliosi, *Reclaiming History*, 1286.

[21] Ibid., 215–16.

[22] Author interview with Brian Latell, February 26, 2012.

INDEX

Note: Abbreviations for full names include LHO for Lee Harvey Oswald; JFK for John F. Kennedy; LBJ for Lyndon Baines Johnson; and RFK for Robert F. Kennedy.

PHOTO CREDITS

Endpapers: Photograph 91-001/314, 1963, Dallas Municipal Archives, City of Dallas; Photograph 91-001/307, 1963, Dallas Municipal Archives, City of Dallas; Photograph, Folder D192, Record Group FBI Files; Released Per P.L.-102-526 (JFK ACT); National Archives at College Park, College Park, MD.

Page xiii: Presidential motorcade, Dallas, Photograph, Record Group 272; Released Per P.L.-102-526 (JFK ACT); National Archives at College Park, College Park, MD.

Page 2: Lee Harvey Oswald, personal photo, Photograph No. 35, Record Group FBI Files; Released Per P.L.-102-526 (JFK ACT); National Archives at College Park, College Park, MD.

Page 3: Texas School Book Depository, Dallas, Photograph Warren Commission Exhibit 477, Records Group Warren Commission Exhibits; Released Per P.L.-102-526 (JFK ACT); National Archives at College Park, College Park, MD.

Page 5: President John F. Kennedy and First Lady Jacqueline Kennedy arriving in Dallas, Photograph, Cecil Stoughton, White House, John F. Kennedy Presidential Library and Museum, Boston.

Page 6: Texas School Book Depository interior, Photograph 91-001/393, 1963, Dallas Municipal Archives, City of Dallas.

Page 9: Marina Oswald, early 1960s, Photograph No. 451, Record Group FBI Files; Released Per P.L.-102-526 (JFK ACT); National Archives at College Park, College Park, MD.

Page 11: Fair Play for Cuba membership card, Photograph 91-001/134, 1963, Dallas Municipal Archives, City of Dallas.

Page 19: Commission Exhibit 143, FBI Exhibit C15, ".38 Caliber Smith & Wesson Revolver," Records Group JFK Assassination Collection; Released Per P.L.-102-526 (JFK ACT); National Archives at College Park, College Park, MD.

Page 28: Jack Ruby at the Carousel Club, Photograph, Warren Commission Exhibit 2425, Records Group Warren Commission Exhibits; Released Per P.L.-102-526 (JFK ACT); National Archives at College Park, College Park, MD.

Page 33: Oswald in custody, Photograph, Gerald L. Hill Exhibit A, Records Group Warren Commission Exhibits; Released Per P.L.-102-526 (JFK ACT); National Archives at College Park, College Park, MD.

Page 34: Texas Theatre, Photograph, Gerald L. Hill Exhibit C, Records Group Warren Commission Exhibits; Released Per P.L.-102-526 (JFK ACT); National Archives at College Park, College Park, MD.

Page 35: Alek Hidell identity cards, Photograph 91-001/155, 1963, Dallas Municipal Archives, City of Dallas.

Page 37: Lyndon Baines Johnson taking the oath of office, Photograph, Cecil Stoughton, White House, John F. Kennedy Presidential Library and Museum, Boston.

Page 39: Basement of the Dallas Municipal Building, Photograph 91-001/406, 1963, Dallas Municipal Archives, City of Dallas.

Page 57: Evidence collected from Ruth Paine home, Photograph, "Pictures shot by FBI Developed by Dallas Police Dept. Oswald's Property," Folder Papers of Jim Garrison; Released Per P.L.-102-526 (JFK ACT); National Archives at College Park, College Park, MD.

Page 63: Ruth Paine home, Photograph, Warren Commission Exhibit 432, "Rear View of Paine Home," Records Group Warren Commission Exhibit; Released Per P.L.-102-526 (JFK ACT); National Archives at College Park, College Park, MD.

Page 64: Fair Play for Cuba flyer, Photograph No. 300, Record Group FBI Files; Released Per P.L.-102-526 (JFK ACT); National Archives at College Park, College Park, MD.

Page 79: Oswald holding daughter June, 1962, Photograph, Folder D33, Record Group FBI Files; Released Per P.L.-102-526 (JFK ACT); National Archives at College Park, College Park, MD.

Page 87: Oswald mug shot, Photograph 91-001/032, 1963, Dallas Municipal Archives, City of Dallas.

Page 88: Lee Harvey Oswald Affidavit, 1963, 1963, Dallas Municipal Archives, City of Dallas.

Page 89: Commission Exhibit Klein's Sporting Goods Artifact, Records Group Warren Commission Exhibits; Released Per P.L.-102-526 (JFK ACT); National Archives at College Park, College Park, MD

Page 100: Oswald's rifle in evidence, Photograph, Warren Commission Exhibit 339, Records Group Warren Commission Exhibits; Released Per P.L.-102-526 (JFK ACT); National Archives at College Park, College Park, MD.

Page 108: Oswald posing with rifle, Photograph, Folder D33, Record Group FBI Files; Released Per P.L.-102-526 (JFK ACT); National Archives at College Park, College Park, MD.

Page 121: Jack Ruby's Western Union receipt, Photograph, Warren Commission Exhibit 2420, Records Group Warren Commission Exhibits; Released Per P.L.-102-526 (JFK ACT); National Archives at College Park, College Park, MD.

Page 130: Oswald autopsy, Photograph 91-001/408, 1963, Dallas Municipal Archives, City of Dallas.

Page 131: Jack Ruby in custody, Photograph, Warren Commission Exhibit 2422, Records Group Warren Commission Exhibits; Released Per P.L.-102-526 (JFK ACT); National Archives at College Park, College Park, MD.

Page 134: Oswald funeral, November 25, 1963, Photograph Warren Commission Exhibit 176, Records Group Warren Commission Exhibits; Released Per P.L.-102-526 (JFK ACT); National Archives at College Park, College Park, MD.

Page 145: Young Oswald, 1950s, Photograph, Record Group FBI Files; Released Per P.L.-102-526 (JFK ACT); National Archives at College Park, College Park, MD.

Page 146T: Oswald and Marina leaving Russia, 1962, Photograph, Record Group FBI Files; Released Per P.L.-102-526 (JFK ACT); National Archives at College Park, College Park, MD.

Page 146C: Marina and Marguerite Oswald, 1962, Photograph, Folder D33, Record Group FBI Files; Released Per P.L.-102-526 (JFK ACT); National Archives at College Park, College Park, MD.

Page 146B: Marina Oswald in Russia, ca. 1961, Photograph, FBI File No. 11, Record Group FBI Files; Released Per P.L.-102-526 (JFK ACT); National Archives at College Park, College Park, MD.

Page 147: Lee with a friend in Minsk, Russia, 1961–62, Photograph, Folder D33, Record Group FBI Files; Released Per P.L.-102-526 (JFK ACT); National Archives at College Park, College Park, MD.

Page 148: LHO Communiqué from Mexico, Photograph Warren Commission Exhibit 15, Records Group Warren Commission Exhibits; Released Per P.L.-102-526 (JFK ACT); National Archives at College Park, College Park, MD.

Page 149T: JFK motorcade, Photograph 91-001/396, 1963, Dallas Municipal Archives, City of Dallas.

Page 149B: Polaroid of JFK limousine speeding off after shots, Photograph, Folder D150, Record Group FBI Files; Released Per P.L.-102-526 (JFK ACT); National Archives at College Park, College Park, MD.

Page 150T: Texas School Book Depository outside view, Photograph 91-001/359, 1963, Dallas Municipal Archives, City of Dallas.

Page 150B: Shooter's view from Texas School Book Depository window, shooter's view, Photograph 91-001/320, 1963, Dallas Municipal Archives, City of Dallas.

Page 151T: Texas School Book Depository, interior view, Photograph 91-001/069, 1963, Dallas Municipal Archives, City of Dallas.

Page 151B: Texas School Book Depository, sniper's nest, Photograph 91-001/379, 1963, Dallas Municipal Archives, City of Dallas.

Page 152: The bus LHO rode during his escape, Photograph, Warren Commission Exhibit 375, Records Group Warren Commission Exhibits; Released Per P.L.-102-526 (JFK ACT); National Archives at College Park, College Park, MD.

Page 153: Officer J. D. Tippit, Photograph 91-001/301, 1963, Dallas Municipal Archives, City of Dallas.

Page 154: Tippit crime scene, Photograph 91-001/021, 1963, Dallas Municipal Archives, City of Dallas.

Page 155: Texas Theatre interior, Photograph 91-001/353, 1963, Dallas Municipal Archives, City of Dallas.

Page 156: Arresting LHO at the Texas Theatre, Photograph, Gerald L. Hill Exhibit C, Records Group Warren Commission Exhibits; Released Per P.L.-102-526 (JFK ACT); National Archives at College Park, College Park, MD.

Page 157L: JFK autopsy report, Photograph, Warren Commission Exhibit 387, Records Group Warren Commission Exhibits; Released Per P.L.-102-526 (JFK ACT); National Archives at College Park, College Park, MD.

Page 157R: JFK autopsy report, Photograph, Warren Commission Exhibit 391, Records Group Warren Commission Exhibits; Released Per P.L.-102-526 (JFK ACT); National Archives at College Park, College Park, MD.

Page 158: LBJ taking the oath of office on *Air Force One,* Photograph, Cecil Stoughton, White House, John F. Kennedy Presidential Library and Museum, Boston.

Page 159: LHO ID cards, Photograph 91-001/132, 1963, Dallas Municipal Archives, City of Dallas.

Page 160: LHO mug shot, Photograph 91-001/084, 1963, Dallas Municipal Archives, City of Dallas.

Page 161: LHO fingerprints, Photograph 91-001/314, 1963, Dallas Municipal Archives, City of Dallas.

Page 162: Jack Ruby in the Dallas Police Department hallway, Photograph, Warren Commission Exhibit 2423, Records Group Warren Commission Exhibits; Released Per P.L.-102-526 (JFK ACT); National Archives at College Park, College Park, MD.

Page 165: Jack Ruby mug shot, Photograph 91-001/035, 1963, Dallas Municipal Archives, City of Dallas.

Page 166: Oswald funeral, November 25, 1963, Photograph Warren Commission Exhibit 176, Records Group Warren Commission Exhibits; Released Per P.L.-102-526 (JFK ACT); National Archives at College Park, College Park, MD.

LEE HARVEY OSWALD: 48 HOURS TO LIVE:

ABOUT THE DOCUMENTARY

President John F. Kennedy has now been dead longer than he lived. Paradoxically, Kennedy's assassination on Friday, November 22, 1963, remains one of the most well-documented and most misunderstood events in American history. Americans remain fascinated by his death, unconvinced by the findings of the Warren Commission, and consumed by conspiracy theories. Of the hundreds of books and dozens of documentaries on the assassination, nearly all have focused on a single question: who shot JFK?

The answers submitted over the past half-century are almost as abundant as the number of pages produced on the subject: the mafia, pro-Castro Cubans, anti-Castro Cubans, the Soviets, the CIA, the FBI, the Secret Service, even Jackie Kennedy herself (!). And the list goes on. Some theories are more intriguing than others to be sure, but nearly all reject the most logical — yet elusive — choice: a lone assassin named Lee Harvey Oswald. The physical and circumstantial evidence leaves little doubt that Oswald pulled the trigger in Dealey Plaza and soon thereafter killed a policeman named J. D. Tippit.

Nevertheless Oswald still remains a mystery.

Surely, part of the reason Oswald remains a mystery is because his own shocking murder on November 24, 1963, forever silenced him. But there are other reasons — beginning with the fact that he introduced himself as a mystery to Dallas police when he was captured one hour and twenty minutes after Kennedy's assassination. Unwilling to reveal his name, officers rifled through the subject's wallet and pulled out two different identification cards with his picture: one for Alek J. Hidell and one for Lee Harvey Oswald.

Over the next two days under intense interrogation, the puzzle surrounding the suspect only became more complicated, leaving an atmosphere thick with paranoia and suspicion: revelations of secret trips to the Cuban and Soviet embassies in Mexico City just weeks prior to November 22, an alleged meeting with the KGB colonel responsible for the Soviet Union's sabotage and assassination programs, a mother claiming her son was really an agent for the U.S. government, and a seedy nightclub owner in the person of Jack Ruby, who eventually gunned Oswald down on live television.

By Monday, November 25, 1963, Oswald was dead and buried, but his emphatic denials of having anything to do with Officer Tippit's murder or John F. Kennedy's assassination — both in the interrogation room and to the world media covering the story — have inspired a heated debate that has endured for five decades: who was Lee Harvey Oswald?

Even to those who were with him for the last forty-eight hours of his life, Oswald remained an almost indefinable figure. FBI agents expressed contempt, dismissing him as "arrogant and argumentative." To the numerous Dallas detectives in the interrogation room, Oswald was in complete control. To the head of Dallas homicide, Captain Will Fritz, who spent more time with the suspect after the shooting than anyone else, Oswald was too good — too skilled at anticipating questions; too quick to deflect probing inquiries; too calm in the face of overwhelming circumstances; and too fearless considering the charges against him. Captain Fritz wondered: Had Oswald received special training in how to deflect police questioning?

Lee Harvey Oswald: 48 Hours to Live seeks to explain the enigmatic Oswald using a new approach. No other documentary has exclusively traced Oswald's actions in the minutes, hours, and days following the events in Dallas. By shifting the focus to that November weekend, we're able to tell a familiar story in an unfamiliar way, providing a refreshing new perspective on Oswald himself, as well as on the Kennedy assassination. Ultimately, the film lays bare the suspect's final two days, revealing why the Dallas police were convinced they had Kennedy's killer.

On his way to the police station after his arrest at the Texas Theatre, an officer asked Oswald whether or not he killed the president. Oswald snidely replied: "You find out for yourself."

Lee Harvey Oswald: 48 Hours to Live eagerly takes up Oswald's fifty-year-old challenge.

For more information visit **www.history.com**